IMAGES
of America

KENNEWICK

WASHINGTON

IN THE DAYS OF STEAM. Here is the steamboat *W.R. Todd*, pictured in 1912, tied up in the foreground while another steamer unloads cargo in the background. In the upper portion of the photo is the Union Pacific Bridge with a train, to the left, belching steam as it crosses high above the Columbia River. The bridge was completed in 1888. Five years earlier, in 1883, Kennewick was nothing but the homestead claim of millwright C.J. Beach, who founded the town. For some years the bulk of Kennewick's population consisted of the bridge workers who labored to span the wide Columbia River. In February of 1888 construction of the bridge was delayed for several months when ice on the river took out a pier. Lengthy repairs were not completed until April. By September, rail traffic was crossing between Kennewick and Pasco. Another challenge confronted by the railroad builders was the tunnel through the crest of the Cascade Mountains. But it, too, was completed in 1888, allowing through service to Puget Sound and the coast beginning in May. (Courtesy of EBCHS)

IMAGES
of America

KENNEWICK

WASHINGTON

Mary Trotter Kion

ARCADIA
PUBLISHING

Published by Arcadia Publishing
Charleston, South Carolina

Library of Congress Catalog Card Number: 2002109927

For all general information contact Arcadia Publishing at:
Telephone 843-853-2070
Fax 843-853-0044
E-Mail sales@arcadiapublishing.com
For customer service and orders:
Toll-Free 1-888-313-2665

Visit us on the Internet at www.arcadiapublishing.com

KENNEWICK, THE TOWN BESIDE THE RIVER IN 1902. This is the earliest known picture of Kennewick. In 1902 the rivers were about to supply everyone with irrigation water, and, as a result of the irrigation being advertised, Kennewick's population jumped from 50 people in 1902 to a whopping 400 in 1903. Many pioneers were well established here by this time. Charles and Sadie Conway, among the earliest, had arrived from Crow Wing, Minnesota. They later recalled that there had been only a few stockmen up and down the river then. Cattle and horses pretty much roamed where they could find forage. One of the first stockmen was Ben Rosecrans, who built a waterwheel and watered a garden and a little orchard he'd set out. In 1888, Frank and I.W. Dudley bought 20,000 acres along the lower Yakima and Columbia Rivers from the Northern Pacific Railroad. This acreage included the town site of Kennewick. Then they incorporated the Yakima Irrigation and Improvement Company to bring the rivers to the dry land and Kennewick was on its way.

4

CONTENTS

ACKNOWLEDGMENTS

I would like to thank the East Benton County Historical Society (EBCHS) for all of their generous assistance and for the loan of many wonderful historical photographs and writings about the early days of Kennewick, Washington.

I am especially grateful to Corene Hulse who, from my first phone call to EBCHS, was a constantly enthusiastic assistant throughout the endless hours of photograph selecting and research. She always seemed to know just the photo I wanted next, often before I knew. Though she claimed to only be doing her job, Corene went far beyond that point. Without her assistance this book might never have been published. I also thank Steve Sandlin, the EBCH Museum curator, for his help with military matters. My respect is extended to the late Neva Bequette for the time and labor she surely put into recording the memories of many early Kennewick pioneers.

My appreciation goes to Sarah Wassell, Arcadia Publishing's acquisition editor for Washington State, for her patience and understanding.

A final and deepest thanks goes to Amber Marie Buchanan, who listened to my dreams, and to my five best friends who waited almost patiently for treats and ear scratchings.

KENNEWICK'S EAST BENTON COUNTY MUSEUM BUILDING. This wonderful building, located at 205 Keewaydin Drive, Kennewick, Washington, houses most of the photos and artifacts seen in this book. The museum holds a wonderful and delightfully varied collection of visual recollections spanning from Kennewick's earliest history to the present day. (Photo courtesy of the author.)

INTRODUCTION

Along one bank of the Columbia River lies a small island. How long this island has existed is beyond knowledge. Whether this island was a part of the results of the devastating eruption of Mount Mazama, a southern Oregon volcano that exploded 6,500 or more years ago, can only be a speculation. But from the beginning of memory this minute oasis in a land of blowing sand and rolling dry sage, covered with nourishing grass and a tangle of other wild plants, has existed.

That the early native people at least traveled through the area where the small green island lived is nearly certain. Their bones and the relics of their lives have been excavated by archaeologists in many locations in the area. In what would become the Kennewick Valley these native people made their homes, created their cultures, and lived their lives according to ancient rules and believes decreed by their gods.

For these Indians the small island was a haven in winter. As the mighty Columbia flowed past for eons upon eons this minute space granted by Mother Earth gave substance, no matter the season, to the horses that belonged to the Native People. And ever since the Indians had acquired horses these magnificent beasts were their wealth. It had always been so, and so they believed it would always be.

The Indians gave their island a name. The name meant 'a grassy place.' They called it *Kin-I-wak*. Today, that same island is known as Clover Island. The town that would some day grow up beside the river and the island would be called Kennewick, first in the Territory of Washington, then in the state of that same name. But this would not happen for many years yet to come.

Change was in the earth-warming Chinook winds that rushed across this empty desert beside the river, even before the year of 1805. But on October 17 and 18 of that year the Corps of Discovery Expedition, led by Captains Meriwether Lewis and William Clark, paused beside the Columbia River to rest from the rigors of their far-reaching journey. Their brief camp was set up just a few miles from where this future city of Kennewick, Washington, would be on the other side of the river. Where Lewis and Clark camped for those two days is now Sacajawea State Park, located where the Snake River joins the Columbia River. The Indians called the Snake River the River *Kimooenim*, meaning the Snake. And here, just above the junction of the Snake and Columbia Rivers the Lewis and Clark Expedition paused to smoke with the native people who had gathered in great numbers. For most, these were the first white men they had ever seen. There would be more—many more.

The Wanapum Indians in the area called the Columbia River *Chiawana*. The name meant 'Big River.' The land that stretched beyond this big river on either side of its banks was a vast arid expanse. Here there were very few small animals or plants usable for food. There was even a lesser amount of material for fire or shelter. And so this Great Columbia Plain remained nearly empty except for a few Indian villages scattered widely apart along the banks of the Columbia, Yakima, and Snake Rivers. What drew people to these rivers, even as far back as pre-historic times, was a bountiful resource that inhabited a mighty waterway—salmon. The rivers teemed with them in their season. And so the People came.

In July of 1811 the natives again saw a white man when British fur trader David Thompson of the North West Company glided his canoe down the Columbia. Like Lewis and Clark, some years earlier, Thompson stopped to smoke with the Indians. He assured them that soon there would be a trading house established here, and expressed his hopes that a trading ship would arrive by sea the following year.

As time passed other white men came and went. Fortunately, some recorded what they saw. One such person was Hudson's Bay employee John Work. In 1824, after traversing the area, he commented in print that "we were like to be choked by dust." A year later, Hudson's Bay Company's governor George Simpson declared the area to be "the most sterile tract country perhaps in North America." And so the descriptions went, leaving scant reason for white settlement until 1883.

In that year the Northern Pacific Railroad track that was being constructed from Spokane to Seattle by way of Yakima reached the Columbia River. A party was sent to locate a suitable place to construct a bridge across this wide expanse of water. After considerable exploration was conducted, with no suitable site located, the party landed on a small island covered with greenery—much later, it became known as Clover Island.

Soon a decision was made to locate the bridge a short distance down river at a place called Cottonwood Landing. The construction crews began to arrive and set up their camps on both sides of the river and in 1884 a survey for a town named Kennewick was made. The railroad bridge construction crews were followed to Kennewick by their families. Soon, other settlers and homesteaders arrived, often traveling from far across the ocean. Some of these early pioneers became business owners and builders, teachers of letters and religion, law enforcers and sometimes outlaws. But in time, Kennewick blossomed in the desert beside the big river, the Columbia.

COLUMBIA RIVER FROM CLOVER ISLAND. Looking through the leafy green of spring that covers Clover Island, the early Native Americans saw the Columbia River much the same as it appears in this early photograph. Though explorers and fur traders had come into their area, Native people were surely startled and concerned when, in 1858, other white men began to appear. These newcomers were miners, passing through from California and Oregon Territory, headed for the gold fields on the Fraser River of British Columbia. A year later, frightening, steam-belching monsters began to glide over the "Big River" as routine steamboat travel on the rivers began. By the 1860s steamboats were carrying men and freight up the Columbia from Portland on their way to the mines to the north and east. For the next 20-some years, the Indians could watch from their island the ever-increasing river traffic. Then the day came that another steam-belching monster invaded their world, only this creature traveled by land and boats such as the *Frederick Billings* ferried the monsters called trains across the water until the railroad bridge was completed. (Courtesy of the author.)

One

LIVING WITH
THE RIVERS

ACROSS THE COLUMBIA RIVER. This view is looking towards Kennewick, across the wide expanse of the Columbia River, from the empty beach that borders the town of Pasco, Washington. Steam rising into the air in the distance gives a feeling of the progress that Kennewick saw throughout the early 1900s and on into the future. (Courtesy of EBCHS.)

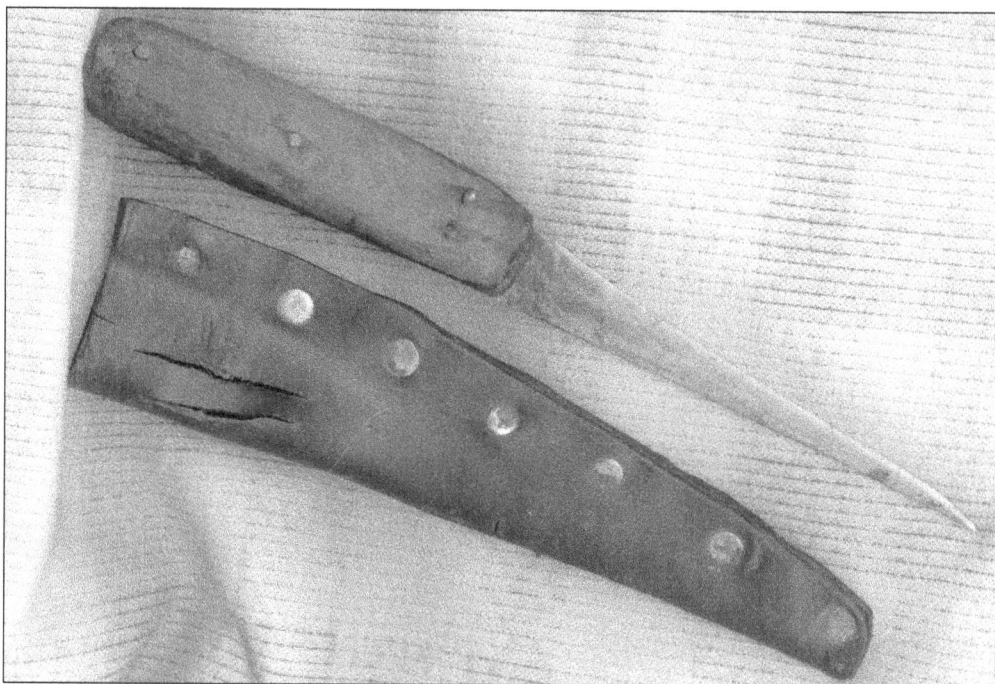

GREEN RIVER KNIFE. This relic of an undetermined earlier time in Kennewick's history was unearthed, from about two feet down in 1980, by the author's son while installing irrigation lines at the base of Badger Mountain just outside of present-day Kennewick's city limits. The Green River knives and similar bladed tools were often carried by mountain men and were common trade items to the Indians. (Courtesy of Jason Troy Kion.)

HUDSON'S BAY STORE. This relic of the past stood at the original site of White Bluffs, Washington. How thrilling it would have been to hear the stories this old building might have told of the past. The placing of a post at White Bluffs by Hudson's Bay was good business—good fur business. From this location a road northeast was laid out in 1863 across the Plain connecting the future Kennewick Valley with Montana and Kootenay routes. (Courtesy of EBCHS.)

DISASTER STRIKES, APRIL 14, 1893. At Wade's Bar, the *Annie Faxton* ended her days on the river when her boiler exploded. Ship's Captain Baughman landed, dazed and hurt, on the bank. His pilot was beheaded by flying wreckage. And though Purser Tappan survived, his bride was thrown into the river where she drowned. A total of eight people were killed. (Courtesy of EBCHS.)

THE *Almota* IN 1897. This ship was built at Celilo Falls in 1876, long before the Northern Pacific Railroad bridge builders arrived in Kennewick. The call of "Steamboat a comin'" seems to have attracted a variety of site-seers. Note the presence of not only passengers but also cowboys and Indians. By the 1860s, steam-powered craft carried men and freight up the Columbia from Portland. The *Almota* was dismantled in 1901. (Courtesy of EBCHS.)

THE *Hercules* IN 1899. This Columbia River sternwheeler surely witnessed early Kennewick's progress as she steamed up and down the river. She may have observed the C.J. Beach family on a Sunday picnic, in 1882, as they paddled their canoe across the Columbia and picked out their homestead site where the future town of Kennewick would someday be established. (Courtesy of EBCHS.)

THE FLOODED COLUMBIA IN 1905. In this year the bridge was damaged by ice flows. In 1894 the Columbia rose to a level higher than had ever been recorded before, overran its banks, and stood three to four feet deep in Kennewick. The floodwaters that were strewn with logs, merchandise, dead horses, cattle, and even a miner's cabin reached up to the tracks on the bridge. (Courtesy of EBCHS.)

THE LAURITZ SMITH FARM. This photo was taken from the Highlands above the railroad tracks in about 1904 or 1905. The Columbia River is shown at the top of the picture. At the time this picture was taken, Ewald Smith and his brothers had five connecting farms along the Columbia River. The Northern Pacific Irrigation canal and the Oregon and Washington Railway and Navigation tracks are in the foreground. The area pictured here is now a part of the freeway between Kennewick and Richland, Washington. Columbia Park now covers the area between the highway and the river. Some 26 years later in 1931, Lauritz Smith or a decent of his would be an 8th grade teacher in the Kennewick School. Also teaching the 8th grade that year with Smith was Carl Precht who had previously, in 1926, been a 6th grade teacher. (Courtesy of EBCHS.)

DOCKED BOAT ON THE SNAKE RIVER. This river enters the Columbia River across from present-day Kennewick. It enters the state at the border between Washington and Idaho at Clarkston. The Indians called the Snake River *Ki-moo-e-nim*. Where it enters the Columbia it was an age-old gathering place for the Nez Perce, Palouse, Walla Walla, Cayuse, Umatilla, and Yakima Indians. (Courtesy of EBCHS.)

THE STEAMBOAT *Gerome* IN 1905. River steamers, such as the *Gerome*, pictured with the Kennewick Band furnishing music, could be chartered for special occasions. Picnic baskets were taken along for a meal, after landing near a grove of trees at the mouth of the Walla Walla River. The steamer *Gerome* ran between Priest Rapids and The Dalles and was headquartered in Kennewick. (Courtesy of EBCHS.)

THE MOUNTAIN GEM AND THE W.R. TODD. They are docked at Kennewick Landing. In 1905 Kennewick became the transfer point on the Columbia between The Dalles and White Bluffs. The boats were running at regular intervals, going as far upriver as the foot of Priest Rapids. That year the *Mountain Gem* was added to the fleet. The *W.R. Todd* plied the river until 1912 when she hit the railroad bridge and sank. (Courtesy of EBCHS.)

THE BIG WASHOUT OF 1907. Living with the rivers was not always easy as the above photo shows. This washout occurred in late winter when snow began to melt. The runoff accumulated behind the 30-foot railroad fill west of town that was not intended to serve as a dam. It gave way when water covered five or six acres and was 25 feet deep against it. Further disaster came into the lives of Kennewick's residents when an eastbound freight ran into the washout. Nine cars were derailed and a dynamite car was left upside down off the tracks. The wrecking crew worked through a long and cold night clearing the tracks. This was followed, in January, with wind, dust, snowstorms, and extreme cold. The drifting ice on the rivers was so bad that the *Richland Flyer* and other small boats were taken from the water and put on skids. Then, in early February, the first Chinook wind of the season hastened the thaw that brought on more flooding. (Courtesy of EBCHS.)

A Second Train Wreck. A couple of weeks following the first train wreck due to the washout, a heavy freight train carrying lumber and shingles, doing from 50 to 60 miles an hour, wrecked at the same place as the first 1907 washout train disaster. Kennewick residents saw 22 cars totally demolished. A 50-foot trestle that had been put in following the first wreck was smashed. Four "hobos" that had been riding in a lumber car were killed. The winter and the derailments caused havoc in the Kennewick area for some time. The Irrigation Company worked hard to get the ditch in shape for the April 1 irrigation season to begin. Telephone service was interrupted and there was a shortage of much needed coal. By March 1, the Columbia River was nearly clear of ice and riverboats were once again serving the population. There was a great quantity of freight to be moved and numerous passengers to transport. (Courtesy of EBCHS.)

ALL DRESSED UP AND GOING DOWN THE RIVER. Seen here are Mabel Smith Mills (Fred) and Dorthea Smith Bruce, in the early 1900s, boating on the Columbia River. It was said that neither of the ladies could swim. Mabel Smith did have other talents, though. In 1907 she was one of four Kennewick students to receive honorable mention as a best all-around student. (Courtesy of EBCHS.)

OREGON AND WASHINGTON RAILWAY AND NAVIGATION OFFICE. Pictured are Ellis Dorothy, agent J.B. Thomas, and Herb Shanafelt. In 1893, *Northwest Magazine* stated that the Northern Pacific Railroad bridge crossed the Columbia River at Kennewick, pointing out that this convenience in conjunction with the Oregon and Washington Railway and Navigation assured that produce from the area was easily shipped to various markets. (Courtesy of EBCHS.)

A ROMANTIC RIDE BESIDE THE RIVER. It is uncertain at the time this picture was taken in 1905, whether Clarence King had yet claimed Inez Church as his bride. They could have also taken a steamboat up river to Priest Rapids. As well that year, the Northern Pacific that crossed the river ran a special train to Portland's Lewis and Clark Exposition for $10 round trip. (Courtesy of EBCHS.)

THE WANISTA, BUILT IN 1908. It was moved to the Kennewick-Pasco crossing in 1910. About that time, James Gavin converted it to steam from gasoline. The ferry sank in 1914, but the owners, C.A. Lundy and Gavin, had it back in operation within a week. Running the ferry wasn't the only business Lundy was involved in. He owned several real estate businesses, managed the telephone company, and was also a farmer. (Courtesy of EBCHS.)

KENNEWICK'S NAMESAKE. In March of 1908 a new boat, *The Kennewick*, was portaged over Celilo Falls. It was to be the fastest steamboat on the Columbia River. The fact that it had passenger sleeper accommodations only added to its acclaim. The *W.R. Todd* was not so fortunate that year. In January she ran aground on a sand bar but the *Mountain Gem* rescued her. (Courtesy of EBCHS.)

ON THE KENNEWICK WATERFRONT IN 1909. This is the North Side of Clover Island. The steamboat in the foreground at the left is the *W.R. Todd*. Next in line is the *Umatilla*. The remaining two boats are unidentified. In this same year the Inland Boat and Machinery Company established a boathouse here after fill was added to the island so that high water would not interfere with business. (Courtesy of EBCHS.)

WRECK OF THE W.R. TODD IN 1912. In February of this year the *Todd* was to replace the *Mountain Gem*. However, disaster struck on June 28 when the *Todd* hit the railroad bridge and sank. A log, submerged at high water time that became caught in the boat's rudder, caused the accident. The *Todd* was never retrieved from its watery grave. (Courtesy of EBCHS.)

MAKING A BIG SPLASH IN 1921. Steam-powered ferries were running between Kennewick and Pasco in the spring when the Columbia River was reaching its crest. The landing was flooded which resulted in probably more than this auto making a splash when it disembarked. By 1921 the number of cars on the roads prompted the state to require all drivers to have licenses. (Courtesy of EBCHS.)

KENNEWICK IN 1923. In January one of the worst storms to ever hit the area occurred. Trees were uprooted and large plate glass windows in Washington Hardware were broken. Disasters continued through that year. There was a blight and scale on the fruit trees and potato crops were infested with Colorado beetles. Some good news came in April when the tractor was introduced to the Kennewick area. Vic Heberlein and M.L. Tucker bought the first one. To make up for earlier crop disasters, both asparagus and strawberries came in well. Hopes were high earlier in the year for government money to assist with the irrigation but in December word came that Kittitas Highline at Ellensburg would get the funds. The rivers also had their troubles this year, in a way. In May, Ted Broughton fell from the O.W.R. & N. bridge scaffold and was swept away. His body was not found until June 7. (Courtesy of EBCHS.)

Two

THIS BOUNTIFUL DESERT

A BOUNTY OF PEARS. Pictured second from the left, wearing a white shirt and necktie, is John J. Rudkin. He came to Kennewick in 1908 as one of the owners of a private company that purchased the Northern Pacific Irrigation canal. He developed the 14,000 acres south and west of Kennewick, and brought water from the Columbia Irrigation Canal to the lower part of "The Highlands." (Courtesy of EBCHS.)

HOP PICKERS IN 1894. These folks are from the Yakimas, Klikitats, Umatillias, and Nez Perce tribes. The rough-stemmed, twining, perennial herb these workers picked is of the mulberry family. Hop gardens existed in France and Germany in the 8th and 9th centuries. These vines, often reaching 25 feet long in a single season, were naturalized in North America in the 17th century. (Courtesy of EBCHS.)

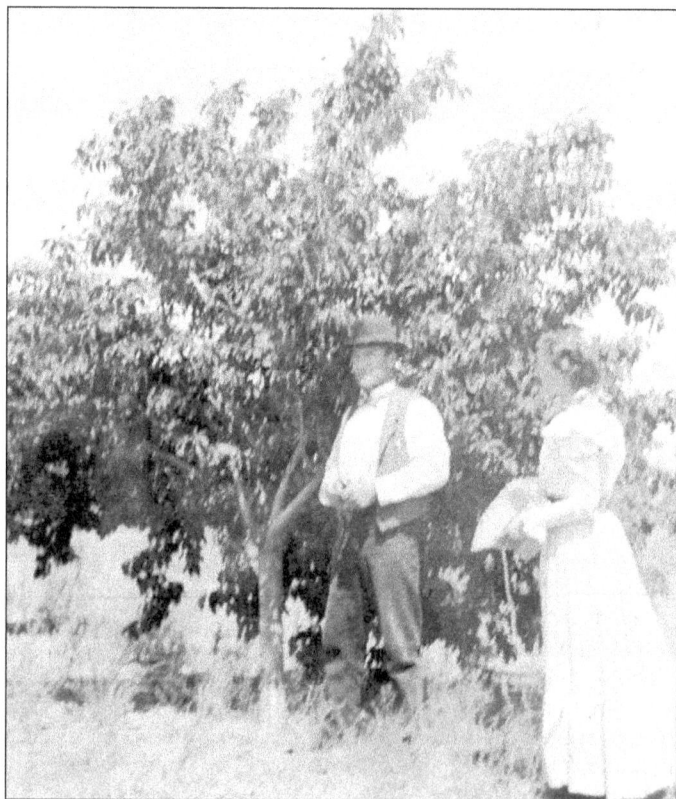

THE BOUNTIFUL CHARLES LUM FARM. The Lums farmed southeast of Kennewick. In 1885 Captain W.P. Gray built the first hotel in Kennewick and Charles Lum was the host. He was also elected as one of the first two school directors for the newly organized school district in 1884. Charles Lum came to Kennewick in 1884 as a bridge contractor for the Northern Pacific Railroad. (Courtesy of EBCHS.)

GEORGE EDWARD HANSEN'S PEACH ORCHARD. Hansen's father-in-law, who came to the U.S. in 1842, is in the center, while Hansen is pictured to the right. The irrigation water that was on its way to the Kennewick Valley by 1902 made orchards such as Hansen's possible and bountiful. Land was not only being planted in peaches but also apples, apricots, pears, plums, and cherries. (Courtesy of EBCHS.)

AT HOME AMONG THE STRAWBERRIES. This is the home of W.H. Collins, built in 1905, and his side-yard strawberry field. Mrs. Collins, in 1907, was a member of the ladies of the Kennewick Cemetery Association. They had a tree-planting day on October 25 that year. They also organized a party for grading the hill leading to the cemetery. Mr. Collins superintended the roadwork for the project. (Courtesy of EBCHS.)

CHERRY HARVEST, 1925. The little boy looking at the camera is five-year-old Kenneth Staley, son of Odin and Georgia Staley. The other children shown are unidentified. Kenneth Staley's grandparents and parents were some of the first Kennewick settlers. His mother, Georgia, was a member of the 1910 Kennewick High School Women's basketball team. His father, Odin, served in World War I. (Courtesy of EBCHS.)

CHARLES SHIVERS' STRAWBERRIES. Mr. Innes is stooped, in the left foreground, wearing a light colored shirt. In the second row, second from the right, is Olive Shivers. Charles Shivers is standing in the background to the left. As early as 1893 strawberry plants in Kennewick were producing. In May of that year they sold for $1 a gallon. More could have been sold had they been available. (Courtesy of EBCHS.)

M.H. CHURCH GAVE KENNEWICK A JUICY FUTURE. In 1913 Mrs. Church put up a batch of juice, without sugar, from her husband's Concord grapes. The sweet nectar was so delicious that Mr. Church decided to bottle the juice and Church Grape Juice Company was born. It became the biggest industry in Kennewick and the first juice factory in the West. (Courtesy of EBCHS.)

GRAPE QUEEN IN **1913.** Francis Olbrich was crowned in 1913 as the Grape Carnival Queen. Other members of the Olbrich family were finding Kennewick bountiful in many ways. About 1910 Joe Olbrich was the owner of the Valley Barn. Electricity became bountiful that year thanks to the Yakima Valley Power Company that spanned the Columbia with a cable on steel towers. (Courtesy of EBCHS.)

KENNEWICK GRAPE FESTIVAL 1911. This is the Twin-Cities Ice and Cold Storage Company's exhibit for 1911. In this year tons of grapes were displayed at the Tabernacle and the Carnival headquarters. The Burns exhibit won the James Hill cup. This was the same year that the first Annual Poultry Show and the Strawberry Festival were held. All of these festivals, combined, were the forerunner of the Benton-Franklin County Fair. (Courtesy of EBCHS.)

THE FOURTH ANNUAL GRAPE CARNIVAL WAS HELD IN 1914. Displayed here is the Silver Cup Award. The cup now resides at the East Benton County Historical Museum in Kennewick, Washington. The 1914 carnival was enlarged to include dry farming exhibits. Professor M.S. Lewis was chairman for this year's carnival. The queen was Fern Ferrel. (Courtesy of EBCHS.)

MARGARET BAXTER O'HEARN, 1921 GRAPE FESTIVAL QUEEN. Margaret is shown with her royal court. These adorable children were members of the Gardner and Fyfe families. Members of the Kennewick Business Girls' Club made Margaret's gown and robe. She was crowned by Mayor Desgranges. The first annual Kennewick Grape Festival was held on September 21 and 22 in 1911 with Nima Hoadley as Queen. (Courtesy of EBCHS.)

APPLE CIDER PRESS. This interesting item resides in the entranceway of the East Benton County Museum. In 1908 land was sold in the Highlands in small tracts. It was believed that if a person owned ten acres of bearing orchard they could make a good living. This land sold for $250 to $500 per acre at the time. In 1912 apples had a good year. (Photo courtesy of the author.)

KENNEWICK IN 1910. Things were looking good in Kennewick by 1910 except for the typhoid fever that was running rampant. There was no hospital and several homes were being used for maternity cases. Dr. Crosby headed up a serious drive for a much-needed hospital but it just didn't happen. That was the bad news. The good news was that in January, Yakima Valley Power spanned the Columbia River with a big cable placed on steel towers, adding 72,000 volts of electricity to Kennewick's supply. Another welcomed item was that in July work began on the Celilo Canal, but fires dampened local spirits. In February a hotel on present-day Canal Drive burned to the ground due to low water pressure. Then in May three businesses and the post office sizzled. The population growth was also hot this year. It was reported that by April the population of Kennewick had doubled within the year with the city limits listing 1,000 persons. (Courtesy of EBCHS.)

SPRING TOOTH HARROW. This reminder of Kennewick's early farming endeavors rests among a landscaped area of natural grasses in front of the East Benton County Historical Museum. It may be still now but in its day it surely turned many a clump of sod, entangled with bunchgrass, where vast golden wheat fields would later grow, such as those on Horse Haven Hills. (Photo courtesy of the author.)

FRANK EMIGH'S HAY FIELD. Emigh grew and sold nine tons to the acre in 1908. A heat wave that summer certainly helped Emigh's strawberries. In 1904, over 1,400 crates of strawberries were packed in the Emigh Packing Shed. The Emigh businesses were so profitable that Frank built an imposing home in Kennewick in 1906. (Courtesy of EBCHS.)

MAYOR H.W. DESGRANGES AND SOME VERY LARGE POTATOES. The potato pot wasn't the only kettle Desgranges had boiling. In 1914, he was chosen manager when the Collins Fruit Exchange joined the Kennewick Fruit Exchange and enlarged the organization. In 1918, when a gas and oil gusher came in on Rattlesnake, many Kennewick businessmen took the plunge. Desgranges was among them. With J.W. Bickers, Guy J.H. Hayden, C.A. Crawford, W.F. Genderson, and O.L. Hansen he incorporated the Highlands Gas and Oil Company. On April 13, 1922, the cornerstone was laid for the new Methodist Church. Unfortunately money for the project ran out in June, and a quick drive was held to raise the additional $12,000 needed to complete the church. Desgranges, now mayor of Kennewick, was among those civic leaders who led the drive. The money was raised and the new church was completed by the end of the year. But it wasn't all business and politics for the mayor. In 1922 he was given the honor of crowning Miss Margaret Baxter as Queen of the Fair. (Courtesy of EBCHS.)

RICHARDS'S HORSE HAVEN RANCH IN 1905. Pictured in front are two women, one of which is Mrs. Wentland. The young girl is her daughter, Grace. The men on the porch are, from left to right, Joe Porter, George Stuible, Ed Layton, unidentified, and Mr. Foster, who appears to be holding a baby. The two boys may be George and Charles Richards. (Courtesy of EBCHS.)

HOW DO YOU DRIVE A TRACTOR? This was the big question in 1913 for these unidentified men who are attending a farmers' meeting to learn this new skill. That year Lee M. Lampson, second row and fourth from the right, became Benton County's first county extension agent and the second county agent in the entire state of Washington. Lampson wrote an agriculture column in the *Kennewick Courier*. (Courtesy of EBCHS.)

KENNEWICK DUST STORM, JULY 1905. Dust may have been bountiful in 1905 but it wasn't the only thing that was plentiful. In a Spokane market that was flooded with California berries, a wholesaler offered $6 for all the fresh berries that could be delivered. One Kennewick grower received $8 a crate. Just after the dust storm, H.C. Mitcham had cantaloupes ripe by July 17. The first crate of Kennewick cantaloupes brought $5 at the Seattle market. It was J.B. Slaugenhaupt's summer to brag: he produced a 50-pound watermelon. Though people around the country may not have realized it, many were eating chickens and eggs that were produced right here in Kennewick's dust-blown oasis in the desert, thanks to Marcus Ware and F.E. DeSellem of the Crescent Chicken Ranch. Something else seemed to be sprouting in 1905. The city's first commercial telephone lines went up and every patron was listed in the new telephone directory. Let the dust blow—Kennewick was doing fine. (Courtesy of EBCHS.)

HARVEST TIME AT WILLIE AMON'S RANCH, 1915. This was a rough year for the farmers around the Kennewick area. Those farming in the Horse Haven Hills hardly got the cost of their wheat seed back at the end of the season. The economy wasn't the only problem. Typhoid was on a rampage and chloride of lime was used in the water supply to protect folks. (Courtesy of EBCHS.)

FARMING IN THE KENNEWICK VALLEY IN 1925. This prosperous-looking farm belonged to Charles and Bell Robertson, pictured far left and center respectfully. The girl is Beulah. Prosperity was not for everyone a few years later in 1932. The Depression was in full swing and Charles, with H.P. Cranmer, headed up Team 4 of the chest drive to solicit cash donations for local relief work. (Courtesy of EBCHS.)

HORSE HAVEN HARVEST CREW IN 1917. Pictured here are Grant Rickman, W.A. Gordan, Clark Blodgett, Ray Larkin, Ed Golland, Al Hendrickson, Frank Larkin, Charles Lee, and Otis Long. These men are reclining on sacks filled with wheat. By 1904 the farmers in the area were producing immense wheat harvests. In July of that year the *Courier* noted that Horse Heaven farmers produced from 40 to 50 bushels to an acre. James Kinney, in 1857, was camping in the area when his horses strayed. Their tracks led up the mountainside and over into an upland plain. There, Kinney located his animals happily munching away at the lush bunchgrass growing there. Truly, it was a haven for horses. Settlers coming to Kennewick began settling the Horse Haven Hills about 1882. Not only was it a haven for domestic horses but also numerous wild horses. These were rounded up and sold, and then the farmers broke up the bunchgrass and planted wheat. By 1905 the hills had been transformed into a vast wheat field. (Courtesy of EBCHS.)

Three

GETTING DOWN TO BUSINESS

INTERIOR OF KENNEWICK HARDWARE AND FURNITURE. Henry, Phil, and Alex Bier owned this early business. It was located on Kennewick Avenue and opened in 1908. Pictured are Henry and Phil Bier, with A.F. Brown. Four years prior to the store's opening, Henry became Kennewick's City Treasurer. In 1907 Alex became a trustee of the volunteer Kennewick Fire Department and Phil was made secretary of the Improvement Club. (Courtesy of EBCHS.)

THE ANTLERS HOTEL ABOUT 1888. It was located on the corner of Front Street and Canal Drive opposite the Northern Pacific railway. Nearly 50 years after this picture was taken Mrs. Reuben Gest, the former Adell Lum, related how her mother, Hattie Bennett, came to Kennewick to run the Antlers Hotel. It was there that Hattie met Charles E. Lum Jr. They were married in 1905. Charles Jr. and Hattie's parents and grandparents were true pioneers. Hattie's grandfather, W.A. Bird, came from Scotland in 1803 to Louisville, Kentucky and later crossed the plains west. Her grandmother, Elisa Bird, crossed the plains westward at the age of nine with her parents in 1847. Charles Lum Sr. came west the first time in 1875. They came to Kennewick in 1884 where they built the Antlers Hotel. The hotel burned down in July of 1912. The persons in front of the hotel are unidentified. (Courtesy of EBCHS.)

THE OLD HOTEL KENNEWICK, ABOUT 1890. Capt. W. P. Gray built the Hotel Kennewick in 1885. C.E. Lum served as the hotel's host. The same year that Gray built the hotel Joseph Dimond was appointed postmaster. Dimond had previously, in 1884, built the first business structure in Kennewick. It was a general merchandising store that catered to the railroad employees. (Courtesy of EBCHS.)

COLUMBIA HOTEL IN 1892. It was built by the Yakima Irrigation and Improvement Company on the corner of present-day Dayton and Columbia Avenue. Mrs. Caroline Klitten bought the $30,000 hotel from Northern Pacific in August of 1903 and established the Emanuel Academy there. It was open only a few months before it burned down. In 1914 Mrs. Klitten took over the local creamery. (Courtesy of EBCHS.)

HEBERLIEN RANCH, A FARMING BUSINESS, 1900. In 1907, W.H. Heberlein acquired the first self-binder sold in the area, which bound grain used for hay. Also in 1907, the Williams hay ranch, that consisted of 94 acres and was managed by G.W. Lane, shipped 25 carloads of alfalfa to market. Lane saw four cuttings made that year, totaling over 490 tons, which were sold for an average price of $11 per ton. Before 1888 the land that would be Kennewick and its surrounding area mainly produced sagebrush, coyotes, and jackrabbits. But that year Frank and I.W. Dudley bought some 20,000 acres of land from the Northern Pacific Railroad, which included the future town site of Kennewick. They then formed and incorporated the Yakima Irrigation and Improvement Company. The idea was to bring water from the rivers to the desert. The first step was a small dam built at Horn Rapids on the Yakima River with a gravity flow ditch that wound its way toward Kennewick. (Courtesy of EBCHS.)

EDWARD SHEPPARD'S COLUMBIA PHARMACY, c. 1903. They also sold wallpaper. Some of youngster Jay Perry's 1904 impressions of the town were jackrabbits running through the brush, swimming in the frigid Columbia River, and a drug store ran by Edward Sheppard. About 1902, H.R. Hanes Drug Store, managed by Edward Sheppard, was the place to buy pharmaceuticals. (Courtesy of EBCHS.)

W.G. KING AND SON GENERAL MERCHANDISE STORE, 1907. The sign near the back door adver-tises "Bread Fresh Daily." Those pictured are: unidentified, W.G. King, Gavin Hamilton, Mr. Barton, Clarence E. King, and E.L. Ely. The King brothers had come to Kennewick from Chi-cago in 1903. In 1907 they bought E. Vansyckle's inventory and took charge of the mercantile and the post office. (Courtesy of EBCHS.)

41

WILLIAM REASON AMON, BANK PRESIDENT.
In 1904 Amon's son, Howard, sold the Exchange Bank to his father. Amon, born in 1846 in Missouri, came to Washington in 1890 where he farmed, went into banking, and married Sarah Downing. The Amon children were Howard, Will, Ruth Amon Williams, Alfred, and Annie, who married I.N. Mueller. Mueller was Kennewick's undertaker. (Courtesy of EBCHS.)

THE EXCHANGE BANK IN 1905. Fred Brighthaup is seen at the window. W.R. Amon is on the right. The bank, with S.H. Amon as president, was one of several new businesses begun between 1902 and 1903. In 1907 the Exchange Bank merged into the First National Bank of Kennewick with W.R. Amon as its president. It was the only National Bank in Benton County. (Courtesy of EBCHS.)

KENNEWICK TRANS-
FER COMPANY OFFICE.
From left to right are
George F. Richard-
son, Flona Rose, and
Father Fred. Richard-
son was the president
of the Commercial
Club in 1907. In
1915 he was elected
Kennewick's mayor
but the following
year, as Kennewick
was experiencing
financial difficulties,
Richardson, along
with three other
of the town's civic
leaders, moved on.
Richardson relo-
cated in Ellensburg
in 1916. (Courtesy
of EBCHS.)

THE H.E. HUNTINGTON CLOTHING STORE IN 1907. It was located in the Kennewick Trading
Company. Business was booming in Kennewick that year. Dr. Schlund, a dentist, opened an
office. It was just in time, too, because George C. Fendler of the O.K. Bottling Works was
producing soda pop. In spite of good business, merchants closed their stores on Christmas
Day. (Courtesy of EBCHS.)

GAS WELLS ON RATTLESNAKE MOUNTAIN. From 1916 through 1920 oil and gas fever was at a high pitch. Drilling was done in several places east of Rattlesnake Mountain. Groups of potential investors and interested citizens came from Portland, Seattle, and Spokane to observe the activity. Even the sheepherders got into the act by using the natural gas flame to warm their beans. (Courtesy of EBCHS.)

E.G. FAIRES DRY GOODS STORE. Mr. Faires and W.A. Morain are shown here in front of the store in 1908. A lot of new businesses opened in Kennewick that year. R. Richardson opened a shoe repair shop while John T. DeGork started a tailoring business. Hayden and Homes had a cigar and confectionery establishment and J.H. Nicholas was the proprietor of a plumbing shop. (Courtesy of EBCHS.)

CONCRETE CONSTRUCTION COMPANY. This was the first cement plant in Kennewick. This business surely must have been profitable due to the steady growth of Kennewick in the town's early years. Between the expansion of the railroads, the constant need and desire for new and more expansive homes, as well as Kennewick's ever increasing business district, concrete was certainly in demand. (Courtesy of EBCHS.)

KING'S GROCERY INTERIOR IN 1909, THE YEAR IT WAS REBUILT. Pictured at center is R.H. Anderson; on the right is W.G. King. King and Son moved into this new, larger department store building on the corner of Pacific and Second Street. The establishment provided public rest rooms and an elevator in the rear of the store. In 1925 King bought out Bert Plowman's life insurance business. (Courtesy of EBCHS.)

THE COURIER PRINT SHOP IN 1909. As early as 1893 there was a weekly newspaper in Kennewick. This was a time when the irrigation canal was coming and the future of Kennewick was looking good. But there were problems with the canal and many of the residences moved on. Unfortunately, Winifred Harper's *Columbian* did not last long. By 1904, the *Columbia Courier* was doing a good business and so was Kennewick. The evidence was in the *Courier's* report in March of that year—in 1904 there were at least 500 persons listed as residents, compared to the 100 listed just 2 years earlier. The *Columbia Courier* became the *Kennewick Courier* on April 28, 1905, with Lauren W. Soth as the new owner. Two years later, in 1907, the *Courier* bought a typewriter. "We operate it with both hands and feet and by means of facial contortion and cuss words," the newspaper announced. In 1909, the *Kennewick Reporter* joined the *Franklin Country Herald*, establishing the *Twin City Reporter*, but it closed before 1911. (Courtesy of EBCHS.)

TILE AND BLOCK FACTORY, 1910. It was owned by H. Christian Puderbough and C. Puder-bough, and was located at present-day 603 E. 3rd Street in Kennewick. In 1921 H. Christian was elected the Master of the Pomona Grange, one of 10 granges established in Benton County by 1921, making a total of about 1,000 grange members. The persons pictured here are unidentified. (Courtesy of EBCHS.)

KENNEWICK LAUNDRY IN 1912. In the front row, from left to right, is Mrs. Jim Wisley, Besie McCinney, Elsie White, Mable Losse, and Orlin Fisher; the back row includes Harry Kennedy, Nellie Ferrell, Mrs. Chapman, and Mr. Chapman. Other major businesses in operation in 1912 were a basket factory, a flourmill, an ice and cold storage plant, a brick and tile factory, a feed mill, and a creamery. (Courtesy of EBCHS.)

47

FRANK SCHUNEMAN, KENNEWICK'S FIRST BLACKSMITH. He came to the area about 1880 to work for the Northern Pacific Railroad. The first Kennewick resident, it is believed, was Sam Fischer, an Indian born at the mouth of the Yakima River in 1854. In 1884, the Potters, Charles Lum, Mrs. Bryson Brown, Jim Anderson, and Mrs. Will F. (Effie Aune) Sonderman arrived. (Courtesy of EBCHS.)

E.R. CARNAHAN'S BLACKSMITH SHOP. Bill Jenkins is shown here. Carnahan's did general blacksmithing as well as wagon and carriage repairing. Built in 1909, this concrete block building located on Front Street was still in use in 1959. Kennewick's business district continued to grow in 1909 with Van Hollenbecke Nursery, a dime theatre, and a millinery store. (Courtesy of EBCHS.)

KENNEWICK VALLEY TELEPHONE COMPANY, c. 1909. It was located at 12 South Benton Street. Pictured, from left to right, are Arthur F. Brown, Grace Richardson, and Lucy Richardson Haurchild. In 1904 a telephone franchise was issued to R.L. Kling, to be built by Arthur Brown. Manager C.A. Lundy reported that 60 orders for telephone service had been made. The first phone lines were strung along the main irrigation ditch so the ditch walker could call for aid if there was a break in the ditch. By mid-1906, lines were extended to Hover and the service was connected to the Bell System. Now, Kennewick folks could make calls to anywhere in the U.S. In 1907 calling hours were extended from 7 a.m. to 9 p.m. When they reached 175 telephones in Kennewick, a 24-hour calling service began and Richland was connected to the telephone service. In 1909 Arthur F. Brown, pictured above, bought the phone system from Twin City Telephone Company and changed the name to Kennewick Valley Telephone Company. (Courtesy of EBCHS.)

KEEPING IN TOUCH. This is the interior of the Kennewick Post Office in about 1913. Pictured are C.E. Hiller, Gordon Moore, and George (Herb) Shanafelt. Hiller began with the post office in 1912. Shanafelt was also proprietor of The Toggery, a men's clothing store, located on N. Auburn Street. In addition, Shanafelt was an agent of the Oregon-Washington Railway and Navigation Company. (Courtesy of EBCHS.)

KENNEWICK IN 1905. Business was busy in this year. Right after the first of the year Northern Pacific put on an addition to their mammoth icehouse, doubling its size. In April the *Columbia Courier* changed hands. It became the *Kennewick Courier* with Lauren Soth as the new owner. M.D. Glover pinned on the marshal's star and received $20 a month for his peace-keeping duties. (Courtesy of EBCHS.)

VALLEY BARN, LIVERY AND DRAY, STORAGE AND BAGGAGE. This picture was taken about 1915 when Joe Olbrich owned the Valley Barn. Nathan Thayer established it in 1902. In 1912, Earl Ferrell and a man named Schnell managed the Valley Barn as a livery stable. Penny Ferrell is shown in the buggy in front of the building. (Courtesy of EBCHS.)

NORTHERN PACIFIC'S VISTA STATION, ABOUT 1908. Shown here, also, is the well pump house and water tank. In 1905, the Northern Pacific had men working to add to their large icehouse in Kennewick. When completed, the building would be double its former size. That same year, the railroad strengthened the bridge and replaced the wooden superstructure with steel. (Courtesy of EBCHS.)

THE FARMER'S EXCHANGE IN THE MID-1920S. In 1918, it was a produce and grocery store but according to research, in 1927 E.G. Lape bought C.C. Williams' interest in the business, and then in 1928, Alfred Amon sold his interest in it to E.G. Lape. A year later, Carl Williams and Alfred Amon bought it from E.G. Lape. At some point, Emerald Silliman became the owner and it has been called the Farmer's Exchange since 1939. It is still run by the Silliman family. (Photo courtesy of EBCHS.)

HAAS BAKERY. Businesses feed one another. In 1920 the bakery was in the building of landowner P.J. Murphy. The Highlands Fruit Company bought 67 acres from Murphy and introduced tractors to orchard owners. Local fruit put into some of the bakery's delights surely fed those learning to drive tractors, as well as to Kennewick's firefighters. In 1925, Al Haas was Kennewick's fire chief. (Courtesy of EBCHS.)

Four

A Place to
Call Home

A.H. Richards Built His Home about 1906. The Richards family is seen here on the porch, at 905 West Grande Ronde in the Garden Tracts, in 1907. As of 1990 this fine home was still standing. Richards farmed some 3,000 acres in the Horse Haven Hills. He was among those, in 1909, who favored the installation of a trolley car. The trolley never found a home in Kennewick. (Courtesy of EBCHS.)

THE HEART OF THE HOMESTEAD. This unidentified Kennewick woman really needs no name—
or she shares the name of all the pioneer women who made homes for their families in Kennewick. As a pioneer woman her true name was Brave, Resourceful, Hard Working, and Loving
just to name a very few. With limited resources she made a comfortable home for her family.
She cooked nourishing meals for the hardworking members of her family. At her blackened
wood or coal burning kitchen range she is checking something that I'm certain was delicious.
The wooden, and probably home-made, ironing board to the right, along with the flat iron rest-
ing on it, tells its own story of the many chores Kennewick women had in common in the late
1800s and early 1900s. Even the family mouse-catcher has found a warm haven in this woman's
domain as it nestles beneath the open oven door. (Courtesy of EBCHS.)

THE TIES THAT BIND. This Kennewick home, constructed from railroad ties about 1882, was the home and property of B. Pratt. These solid walls must have kept the Pratt family warm in winter. Also adding to the family's comfort are two chimneys and real glass in the windows. There is little history concerning these early homesteaders but the name Pratt enters Kennewick's later history. (Courtesy of EBCHS.)

THE LAND WHERE THE BEACH FAMILY MADE A HOME. This house was located on the Beach property next to the Northern Pacific Railroad Bridge. About 1903 Beach's Livery and Feed opened in Kennewick, renting transportation to those seeking land in the area. But it wasn't all work for the Beach family. In 1904 a baseball team was organized and Harry Beach was on the team. (Courtesy of EBCHS.)

THE J.J. SERCOMBE HOME, BUILT IN 1902. It was located on East 3rd Avenue. After moving from Idaho, Sercombe purchased land in 1903 on which to raise strawberries and helped bring in the first irrigation. In 1905 Sercombe had one of the largest strawberry crops in Kennewick. In 1913, as a member of the Businessmen's Club of Kennewick, he helped form a Bureau of Marketing. (Courtesy of EBCHS.)

THE AMOS JOHNSON HOME AND OUT BUILDINGS, c. 1904. At the time this picture was taken Kennewick was booming. A telephone franchise was issued this year and sidewalks were planned. In March 1,000 trees were planted. Even dogs and other stray animals could feel at home in Kennewick, as a pound for stray stock had been built to save the new trees. (Courtesy of EBCHS.)

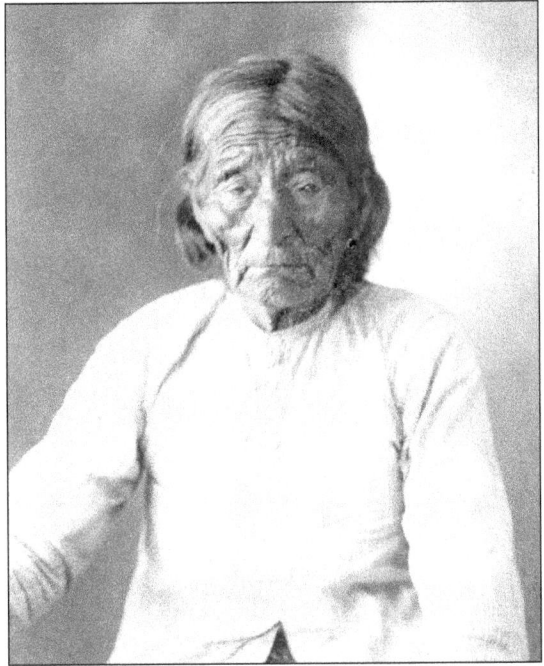

KENNEWICK WAS HIS HOME BEFORE THERE WAS A KENNEWICK. This picture was taken in 1905 when this elderly Yakima gentleman was 104, indicating he was born in 1801. Perhaps in later years he recalled the arrival of Lewis and Clark. Though he was just a toddler of two or three years, his memories may have derived from stories told around the tepee fire on a winter's night. (Courtesy of EBCHS.)

JUDGE G.F. RICHARDSON'S HOME ON AUBURN STREET. Richardson owned Kennewick Transfer, was a police judge, and served two terms as Kennewick's mayor. From left under the windows is Flora Richardson with G.F. Richardson Jr. seated on the steps. The standing man is unknown. Jesse Rose is seated. At the end of the porch is G.F. Richardson Sr. with daughter Lois. (Courtesy of EBCHS.)

HOME ON THE RANGE, OR ANYWHERE THE HORSES PULL IT. Ed Layton owned this unusual wagon home where sheepherder Elgy Maury lived in 1905. It was also used as a cookhouse for harvest crews. Sometime before 1901 Layton settled on Jump-Off Joe, south of Kennewick, where wild horses once roamed. The lower slopes of the 2,196-foot high hill became wheat fields.

HOME OF MR. AND MRS. A.V. MCREYNOLDS. He built this house about 1906, on the corner of Kennewick Avenue and Fruitland where Kennewick Flower Shop is located today. Of the 65 to 70 new homes built in Kennewick that year the McReynolds home was considered one of the most valuable. The house on the left is still standing. A.V. and Sarah McReynolds are in the picture. (Courtesy of EBCHS.)

FRANK EMIGH'S HOME, c. 1906. Shown are Mr. and Mrs. Emigh and their daughter. Around 1902, Emigh was manager of the St. Paul and Tacoma Lumberyard. In a single season over 1,400 crates of strawberries were packed at the Emigh packing shed. His hay fields in 1908 averaged nine tons per acre. Frank was making a good home for his family in Kennewick. (Courtesy of EBCHS.)

DR. CROSBY'S HOME, ABOUT 1906. It was located at 108 East First Avenue. He practiced medicine in Kennewick from 1908–1919. In 1910 there was a typhoid epidemic. There was no hospital in Kennewick at that time and Dr. Crosby headed a drive for one. Unfortunately, a hospital was yet to have a home in Kennewick. At the end of WWI, Captain Crosby returned home and continued to practice medicine. (Courtesy of EBCHS.)

KENNEWICK TOWN. There is a hint of the changing of times about this scene with both horse-drawn conveyances and motor vehicles pulled up along the curbs. It appears that a parade of some sort is in progress, complete with sign-carrying and band music. It could be political with the men spiffed up in suits and the women sporting their best bonnets. (Courtesy of EBCHS.)

L.E. JOHNSON HOME, c. 1906. This home is still standing at 504 West Kennewick Avenue. The Johnsons came to Kennewick in 1905; Johnson was Kennewick's mayor in 1907. He was also a director in the Yakima Valley Publicity League as a representative of the Commercial Club. In addition, he was cashier for the newly formed First National Bank of Kennewick that year. (Courtesy of EBCHS.)

60

THIS CHURCH ONCE SHARED THE HOME OF A SALOON AND DANCE HALL. This was the Methodist Church in Kennewick in 1906 and was Kennewick's first Methodist Church. It was located on the corner of today's Kennewick Avenue and Dayton Street. Prior to it being built, services were first held in the schoolhouse. Later, they were held in the upper room of the Aiken building. A saloon was on the main floor of the building and the area above it was used as a dance hall on Saturday nights. On Sunday mornings the dance hall was converted and was used for church services. When W.R. Amon came to Kennewick to take over the bank he was appalled at the idea of the church sharing premises with a saloon and dance hall. Consequently, Amon led a drive to raise money for building a church. To assist, his son Howard donated two corner lots while an additional five lots were acquired. On April 23, 1905, services opened in the First Methodist Church in Kennewick. (Courtesy of EBCHS.)

C.A. LUNDY HOME, c. 1907. It was located at the corner of Metaline and Jean Streets, near the Columbia River. The house was still standing, as of 1990. Around 1902 Lundy was not only making his home in Kennewick, he was in the business of selling homes and land. His real estate business was one of five that had sprung up about that time. (Courtesy of EBCHS.)

WILL SONDERMAN'S HOME IN 1908. From left to right are daughters Julie and Jessie with Mrs. Effie Aune Sonderman holding son Bud. Effie came west in 1884 at age five. With her mother she traveled by emigrant train to join Effie's father, Charles Aune, who was a lineman for the Northern Pacific Railroad in the Columbia River Valley. Effie married Willie Sonderman ten years later. (Courtesy of EBCHS.)

HOME SWEET TENT. This was the 1908 home of Mr. and Mrs. G.A. Quast, who started a fruit ranch where the Eagles Hall on Fruitland Avenue now stands. Mr. Quast was a ditch rider for the Kennewick Irrigation district. Their son, Nelson, was an outstanding senior graduate from Kennewick High School in 1940. In 1942 he was reported missing in action in the Philippines. (Courtesy of EBCHS.)

THE CATHOLIC CHURCH IN 1911. It was located at the corners of Washington Avenue and Second Street. According to *The Courier*, published by the East Benton County Historical Society, a Catholic Mission was established in Kennewick by the Diocese bishop with 12 to 14 families first attending. In 1920 Father Feige became its first resident priest. (Courtesy of EBCHS.)

A Home For Trees Along the Columbia River. In 1912 Arbor Day was a total business holiday with the whole community turning out to plant ten miles of trees along the Columbia. Also that year it was hoped that the Benton County seat would find a home in Kennewick. Though Kennewick received 55 percent of the votes, 60 percent was required and the seat went to Prosser. (Courtesy of EBCHS.)

Lee and Lottie Lampson at Home in 1916. This was their first home in Kennewick. They are seen here on the porch with 4-H club members from Pullman, Washington. Lottie recalled that, in 1922, Kennewick women served over 500 meals in the new Methodist Church after the opening of the new Auto Bridge over the Columbia River. She was the daughter of Ole J. Holton. (Courtesy of EBCHS.)

Five

THAT'S ENTERTAINMENT

KENNEWICK BAND IN 1904. Professor George Joselyn was the bandleader. Band members are unidentified. This same year Mr. Eakin's Opera House was kept busy. Other entertainment that year included a performance by Alexander Brothers Plantation Minstrels, a Box Social given by the Junior League, and a Thanksgiving "bash" given by the Independent Order of Bachelors. The Kennewick Orchestra made its first public appearance. (Courtesy of EBCHS.)

TAKING TIME OUT FOR A PICNIC IN 1895. Seen here are members of two of the oldest Kennewick families, the Lums and Stuibles. Times in Kennewick were a little rough about then and this simple form of entertainment seems just right. After a major break in the irrigation canal the Lums and the Stuibles lost much of their orchards. Individual members are not identified. (Courtesy of EBCHS.)

EARLY PIONEERS ON A PICNIC IN 1900. Charles E. Lum Sr. and his wife, Almyra, came to Kennewick in 1884. He was a pioneer road and bridge builder, and served in the state legislature. He assisted with the first hotel in Kennewick, the Antlers Hotel. Charles Sr. and Almyra were married in 1873, the day before her 18th birthday. Individual family members and friends are unidentified. (Courtesy of EBCHS.)

SAILING OVER THE BOUNDING CO-
LUMBIA IN 1910. Seen here, seated
in the rowboat, are Ralph Reed and
Cora Sercombe. Pete Tripp is in his
sailboat. The two women with him
are unidentified. Cora Sercombe was
a 1909 graduate of Kennewick High
School, and Tripp was a member of
the Kennewick Band in 1907. (Courtesy of EBCHS.)

SOME PRETTY COOL
ENTERTAINMENT. Ice-
skating on a pond near
Clover Island in 1914
was fun and a good way
to stay warm. Let others
enjoy their autos, horses,
and boats—these skaters
had no need for wheels,
sails, or saddles. Two
good feet and a pair of
ice skates were all that
was necessary to have
fun. The skaters are
unidentified. (Courtesy
of EBCHS.)

WHAT THE FUN OF SKATING AND BOATING CAN LEAD TO—A WEDDING. Seen here on their wedding day are the newly united Mr. and Mrs. J.W. "Sam" Root. Clara, the former Miss Anderson, was born in the Horse Heaven Hills in 1885. Sam and Clara had one child, Margaret, who years later at her own wedding became Mrs. Beightol. (Courtesy of EBCHS.)

THE EVANGELICAL LUTHERAN CHURCH. Churches are always a good, clean source of fun. The Reverend O.C. Helleckson of Genesse, Idaho organized this church on November 26, 1904. It was given the name of the Kennewick Evangelical Lutheran by the charter members. These members were Helleckson, L.A. Tweedt, Hans C. Tweedt, R.C. Miller, C. Olbeg, A. Halverson, Laurtiz Smith, Ingwall Smith, and Lars Erickson. (Courtesy of EBCHS.)

CHRISTMAS AT THE J.H. SIEGFRIED HOME IN 1914. Little Bob and Joseph Siegfried must have had a wonderful time deciding what to play with first from the looks of the assortment of toys under their Christmas tree. Among other toys seen here are, pictured from left to right, a windmill with tripod-like legs, a child's car, a train on the floor, and a hobby horse. This tree appears to be strung with electric lights, even at this early date. It is possible, since Mr. Siegfried was appointed superintendent of Pacific Power and Light in 1912. It wasn't all work, for J.H. Siegfried. One choice of entertainment for him must have been golf as he was elected president of the Golf Club in 1927. Previously, in 1922, the Siegfried home acquired a new form of entertainment. They were the first in Kennewick to have a radio in their home. Mrs. Siegfried surely found considerable enjoyment that same year when Mrs. D.G. Rodgers put in a beauty parlor and an exclusive ladies' shop. (Courtesy of EBCHS.)

THIS KID CAR WAS CALLED AN IRISH-MAIL. Pictured here is one of the Siegfried boys riding the car seen under the Siegfried's Christmas tree in the previous picture. Called an Irish-Mail, the car was given to Bob and Joseph Siegfried for Christmas in 1914. Though the car was bought new, it was handmade. It was equipped with four spoke wheels encased in solid rubber tires. It has a wooden steering wheel and a wooden seat that is 20 inches long by $8^3/4$ inches wide. Brakes, which were operated by a lever on the right side, were also installed on the car. The car itself is 39 inches long with a total width of 18 inches. It was, and still is, an amazing piece of craftmanship. The Irish-Mail can be seen on display at the East Benton County Historical Museum at 205 Keewaydin Drive in Kennewick. (Courtesy of EBCHS.)

COYOTE CLUB MEMBERS AND THEIR MASCOT, FEBRUARY 11, 1914. Pictured, left to right, are A.R. Garner, E.C. Tripp, William Muncey, Guy Haydon, Doc Spalding, Larry Marks, Harry Breed, John Brog, Harry Vebber, Ernest Kolb, Frank Beulley, unidentified, L.E. Johnson, Kit Gifford, Dirk Davis, ? Jeffery, Bert Cole, and ? Reed. The dog is unidentified, but cute. Tripp was owner of Tripp's Pool Room—oh what fun. (Courtesy of EBCHS.)

MODEL T CAMPING. These unidentified Kennewick folks are ready for a camping trip in July of 1919. The camping necessities haven't changed much since the "good old days." Even then, campers carried tents, bedding, food, and plenty of water. A boon to campers and other outdoor folk had come in 1907 when President Roosevelt set aside 148 million acres as national forest. (Courtesy of EBCHS.)

PESKY JACKRABBITS PROVIDED ENTERTAINMENT IN 1907. Shown here with their catch are, from left to right, Henry W. 'Bat' Nelson, I.N. Mueller, Lewis Tweet, A.V. McReynolds and ? Nelson. In Kennewick's early years, New Year's Day was often celebrated with a "Jack Rabbit Drive" near the Horse Haven Hills. Waldo Gerards recalled a bridge across the irrigation canal on his father's place where, at night, the rabbits would cross over to enjoy a midnight snack of alfalfa. Not so fun for the Gerards and others were the rabbit-damaged fruit trees. Where there were no bridges to cross the canal the rabbits evidently enjoyed a late night swim across the water. The drives usually ended at noon at the Finley Grange Hall, where the womenfolk had prepared a big dinner for everyone to enjoy. Henry 'Bat' Nelson had a lumberyard in Kennewick in 1918, as was mentioned in a letter he received from his friend Odin 'Dutch' Staley. Odin was enjoying a uniformed and lengthy stay in France, at the time, during World War I. (Courtesy of EBCHS.)

HUNTING FOR FISH OR FISHING FOR BIRDS?
Wilmont Gravenslund, at the far right,
and his unidentified grinning friends, all
wearing waders and carrying guns, seem to
be well equipped. Whether their inten-
tion was to wade in and shoot fish or shoot
birds over the water can only be guessed at.
But it seems that this day was for the birds.
(Courtesy of EBCHS.)

STEAMBOATS, JOHN GATES AND ALMONTA, ON THE SNAKE RIVER. Seven big steamers had been added to the O.S.N. fleet by 1878. The *John Gates* was one of them. The others were the *Harvest Queen*, *R.R. Thompson*, *Spokane*, *Annie Faxon*, and the *Wide West*. It is believed that the *John Gates* was the first boat up the Snake River. (Courtesy of EBCHS.)

KENNEWICK BAND. In 1905 the first two babies born in Benton County were from Kennewick. One of them was Royce "Pete" Tripp, who would be a future Kennewick band member, as seen here in 1912. Tripp is the youngster to the far right in front of the first step holding a drum. On the first step, third from the right, is Frank Beste. The other band members are unidentified. (Courtesy of EBCHS.)

THE KENNEWICK HIGH SCHOOL GIRL'S BASKETBALL TEAM, 1909. Pictured, from left to right, are Nellie Hoadley, Effie Oliver, Jessie Perry, Georgia Staley, Jessie Falsom, Bernice Griffith, and Coach Lynn Shanafelt. Nellie Hoadley, who became Mrs. Garber, in later years recalled the excitement of the Kennewick "Shoot Out" that occurred in 1906. Bernice Griffith was a 1909 Kennewick High School graduate. (Courtesy of EBCHS.)

KENNEWICK HIGH SCHOOL'S FOOTBALL TEAM IN 1909. Pictured, from left to right, are: (back row) Coach H. Groom, Marvin Carnahan, Archie Copeland, unidentified, Louis Annis, Lyle Johnson, Clint Oliver, and Professor Lewis; (middle row) Guy Story, Earl Larken, unidentified, and Harold Oliver; (front row) ? Smith, ? Erickson, ? Laird, and Floyd Bowers. (Courtesy of EBCHS.)

THOSE BERRYPICKIN' BASEBALL PLAYERS. In 1911, Kennewick's baseball team was called "The Berrypickers." They beat the Wallula-Attailia team 11 to 1 with a near shutout by pitcher Larkin. Baseball had been grand fun in the Kennewick area since about 1906. In that earlier year the Horse Heaven Hustlers took on the Kennewick Sand Snufflers. Later that summer Kennewick trounced Pasco, 13-9. (Courtesy of EBCHS.)

FOR THE *Love* OF TENNIS, ON JANUARY 14, 1912. The location of this tennis match was at Everett Street and Kennewick Avenue. Pictured here at the far left is Dr. Crosby. Dr. Spaulding is third from left with a tennis racket, white shirt, and tie. T.C. Brown is on horseback while Clarence King, in the center and right of the horse, is pushing a baby carriage. Guy Harper is shown, second from the right, with a tennis racket and hitting backhand. On the far right is Ellis Dorothy. The young boy is Gene Spaulding at 4 years old. Gene was the only child of Doctor L.G. and Mrs. Adelaide Spaulding. In 1916 Doctor Spalding and his son enjoyed the novelty of auto touring. In August of that year they returned from a 1,100-mile trip across the Cascades to Seattle, which also took them to Portland. In 1920 Brown became the new owner of Beste's Tire Shop to serve those who found their entertainment in automobile driving. (Courtesy of EBCHS.)

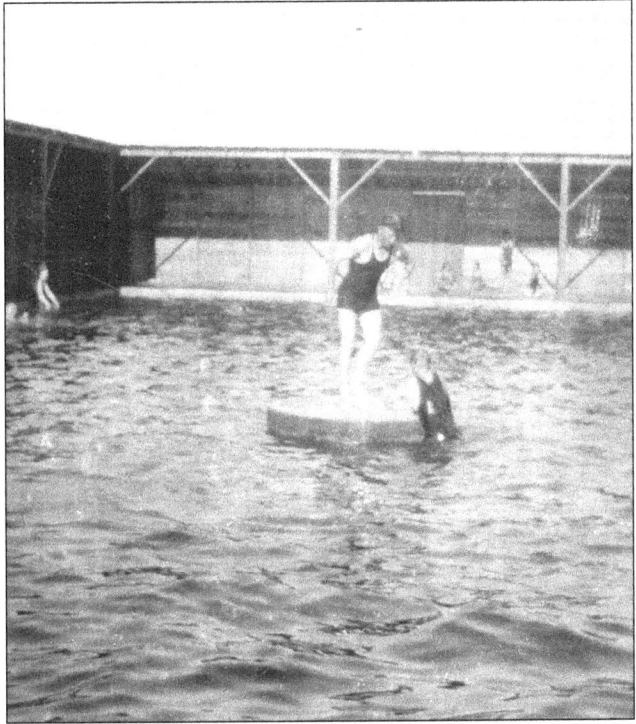

BATHING BEAUTIES OF KENNE-
WICK. What could have been
more fun on a hot day in Kennewick for these two unidentified women? This was Ken-
newick's first swimming pool.
Though it was a private pool,
it was for public use. It was located on Washington Street as
you go out to Clover Island on
the left. (Courtesy of EBCHS.)

KENNEWICK AVENUE. In this early photo, towering trees do not block the view of the river
as they do today. Pictured here are very small trees lining the sidewalk. Some of them still
shade this historical Kennewick byway. The view is to the west, including the residential
area of Fruitland and Everett Streets where, by 1905, some of the 1,011 residents enjoyed
living in Kennewick. (Courtesy of EBCHS.)

77

PUTTING ON A PLAY. Lottie Lampson, wife of Lee Lampson, is seen here with her unidentified students at the Buena Vista School in 1912, providing some special entertainment. More theatrics were on the program in Kennewick that year when the *Roses Maiden* was performed and Kennewick school system contracted with the Pacific Lyceum for lectures, literary presentations, poetry readings, and musical numbers to be performed. (Courtesy of EBCHS.)

SHE STOOPS TO CONQUER. Seen above is a scene from the 1913 Kennewick High School play. The performers are unidentified. Other entertainment that year included a July 4th tennis match and the Grape Festival that sponsored a "Perfect Baby Contest." Combining business with fun was E.A. Pinkney who established a confectionery store. But for the most fun that year, there was a white Christmas. (Courtesy of EBCHS.)

THE PRINCES THEATER, 1915. This was Kennewick's first movie theater. From left to right are Bill Gravenslund, R.L. Banta, Mrs. Banta, Stella Hanson, and Guy Johnson. The poster advertises "The Last Performance." To further enhance theatrical entertainment, in April of 1922 M.W. Mattecheck installed a radio, then called a "Radiophone," in his theater. In 1919 Mattecheck was made president of Kennewick's Commercial Club. (Courtesy of EBCHS.)

THE OLD SWIMMING HOLE. This was the earthen dam to hold spring run off for irrigation. It was called Elliotts Lake, named for the owner of the land. The sign (insert) didn't do much to keep swimmers out. The lake was cold and deep with no sides to walk on or climb out of. In winter it was often used for ice-skating. (Courtesy of EBCHS.)

Gas Wells, a New Form of Entertainment. Between 1914 and 1920 folks enjoyed hitching up the buggy, or starting the auto, and driving up on Rattlesnake Mountain. There they watched, as pictured above, gas wells being drilled. The Roe Ranch on Rattlesnake Mountain was where the excitement began. On July 16, 1914, the Clark Brothers and Klein filed oil gusher claims but they proved to be false. But the fun wasn't over. In June of 1915, Kline, Clark, and McPhee planned another drilling. By 1916 the entertainment on Rattlesnake was taking on the aspect of a gas-drilling circus. The Walla Walla Gas Company was hauling in lumber and machinery to drill with a larger rig. California Oil Company started drilling, as did the Yakima Natural Gas and Oil Company. Soon Walla Walla Gas, Oil, and Pipe Company got into the act. And still more companies were coming in. One came from as far away as Texas. But that year all the wells on Horse Haven eventually flooded out and had to be capped. (Courtesy of EBCHS.)

Six

Law, Leaders, and Outlaws

Kennewick's First Fire Department in 1912. Members of the fire department are posed here in front of the old Kennewick Hardware Building. Some of the gentlemen in the picture are Cy Smock, Phil Bier, Ernie Kolb, Louie Tweedt, Ed Sheppard, J.J. Reed, Allan Tripp, and Postmaster Scott. In May of 1910 a fire destroyed the post office, Pacific Transfer Office, and Richardson's Shoe Store. (Courtesy of EBCHS.)

CHARLES AUNE AND HIS NORTHERN PACIFIC RAILROAD TIME PASS. In 1886 Aune became the first marshal in the Territory of Washington. He came to the valley in 1883 to work as a lineman for the Northern Pacific Railroad. He was one of the first to stay and raise a family here. Their home stood near the Old Military Road that followed the bank of the Columbia. (Courtesy of EBCHS.)

KENNEWICK JAIL SOMETIME AFTER 1905. M.D. Glover became marshal the following year. He received $20 a month for his services. After Glover was sworn in, a warrant of $120 was drawn for a lot on which to build the jail. It was noted that Glover did more for the city in a few months than had been accomplished since Kennewick had begun. (Courtesy of EBCHS.)

"SHOOTOUT" DEPUTY, JOE HOLZHER. On Halloween evening in 1906, a gun battle occurred in Kennewick. It came to be known as the "Shootout at Poplar Grove." At its conclusion four men were dead, including Holzher. A fifth man was seriously wounded. The previous day, October 30, two outlaws burglarized the Tull and Godwin's General Merchandise and the Kennewick Hardware Company. Mrs. R.H. Anderson was an eyewitness to the robbery performed by Jacob "Jake" Lake, who some believed was an ex-convict from Walla Walla. With Lake was his sidekick Kid Barker. After Mrs. Anderson's husband sounded the alarm Marshall Mike Glover and Mr. Tull hastened to a hobo jungle located at the end of the railway bridge. There they encountered two men. Sheriff A.G. McNeill, accompanied by Deputy Holzhey and Harry Roseman, met Marshall Glover and Tull. In a grove of trees one of the suspects was standing with his rifle. He threatened the four men, then opened fire. Roseman, unarmed and now a witness to Holzhey's murder, ran for safety. (Courtesy of EBCHS.)

MARSHAL MIKE GLOVER. He was marshal at the time of the shootout. As Harry Roseman ran for cover, he saw that Deputy Holzhey and Marshal Glover had been hit. McNeill, now wounded, discharged all his bullets and also retreated. With Glover and outlaw Lake now dead, Roseman took McNeill back to town where a posse was formed. Kid Barker was still at large. (Courtesy of EBCHS.)

KID BARKER. He was thought to be about 18 when he surrendered after the shootout and admitted to a part of the shooting. He was jailed to prevent a lynching, and then was hurried off to Prosser on the early train. Barker was charged with murder but he never went to trial. He escaped from Benton County jail several months later and was never heard of again. (Courtesy of EBCHS.)

SHERIFF A.G. McNEILL. He was seriously wounded during the shootout. To die as a result of the shootout was Forrest Perry, who was an innocent member of the volunteer posse. Earlier that year McNeill had arrested George Dymond, one of the most desperate criminals in the northwest and the leader of a gang of horse thieves. McNeill served as sheriff from 1906–1910 and from 1912–1914. (Courtesy of EBCHS.)

KENNEWICK IN 1905, ONE YEAR BEFORE THE FAMED "SHOOTOUT." Laws were being made and enforced. It was now against the law to drive teams or lead horses across the new wooden sidewalks. Also, females were no longer allowed to enter saloons or wine houses. Bartenders were now forbidden by law from serving or allowing women to drink in any public house. (Courtesy of EBCHS.)

L.C. Rolph Was Sheriff From 1918–1920. The 1918 vigilante uprising in the Kennewick area made his time in office difficult. The vigilantes organized to harass German-speaking families. They arrested August Huss of Finley for storing four sacks of flour for which he had traded his produce. On April 18th the vigilantes made a fire of all the German language textbooks they could find. (Courtesy of EBCHS.)

James Shepherd, Kennewick's Sheriff From 1920 to 1930. During Shepherd's years as sheriff, Kennewick continued to grow. Her 1920 population reached 1,684 persons. The berry crop that year set a record and there was more excitement in the gas fields. The new Auto Bridge between Kennewick and Pasco was completed in 1922, and in 1923 the box factory turned out about 5,000 boxes a day. (Courtesy of EBCHS.)

SHERIFF C.E. DUFFY. Duffy enters our story as one of six applicants for county sheriff in 1934. According to one research source, James Shepherd, also an applicant, was sheriff at the time. Previously, in 1922, Duffy endeavored to present Kennewick as a tourist attraction by installing toilets, showers, and camp stoves in Kennewick's first tourist camp, advertised as being on the Yellowstone Trail. (Courtesy of EBCHS.)

ALFRED C. AMON. One law in early Kennewick seemed to have been that everyone must come from somewhere else. It was certainly true for Alfred C. Amon, who later became Kennewick's mayor. The same year, 1884, that a survey was being made for a town named "Kenewick," Amon was born in a log cabin in an area of Oregon known as Centerville, now called Athena. (Courtesy of EBCHS.)

ED COULSON, KENNEWICK'S FIRST FIRE CHIEF, 1906. Fires were a great dread in the early days of any town. Kennewick was no different. On February 16, 1910 the Columbia Hotel on Front Street (present-day Canal Drive) burned to the ground. Spike Farrel, the fire chief at that time, assisted by E.D. Taylor, the hotel's proprietor, evacuated the building. (Courtesy of EBCHS.)

KENNEWICK'S FIRST MOTORIZED FIRE TRUCK. It was a 1922 American La France. In August Kennewick's firemen and their new truck saved the new bridge approach when it caught fire. It was said that the new fire truck crossed to Clover Island through several feet of water, just as though it was a motorboat. However, Harvey Hendricks' shoe-repair shop burned in May. (Courtesy of EBCHS.)

JOHN EICHNER OF THE KENNEWICK FIRE DEPARTMENT IN 1906. Eichner, wearing a fire helmet, with several unidentified persons, is seen here with fire equipment in front of Edward Sheppard's Columbia Pharmacy. In this year, Kennewick set fire limits and made regulations as to erection, alteration, repair, and removal of buildings. A new water pump was installed that could produce 500 gallons of water per minute. After street hydrants were installed all that was needed was for Columbia Basin Water, Light, and Power to announce that it was ready. This was also the year that Kennewick bought a new chemical fire engine that cost $750, and equipment including hose, nozzle, and cart. By 1907 a volunteer fire department had been fully organized with 24 members. The fire fighters got a chance to try out all their new equipment when, at 2:00 a.m., the westbound freight discovered that the Northern Pacific railroad bridge was on fire. The fire was put out and by daylight all repairs had been made. (Courtesy of EBCHS.)

ENVELOPE ADDRESSED TO TEHE, WASHINGTON TERRITORY, IN 1887. It is uncertain why Kennewick's post office was called Tehe at one time. As Charles Conway declared when he first saw the place, "It was no laughing matter." The Conways, anticipating an Eden, landed in the midst of sand and dry sagebrush during a sever dust storm, such as the area is still famous for. (Courtesy of EBCHS.)

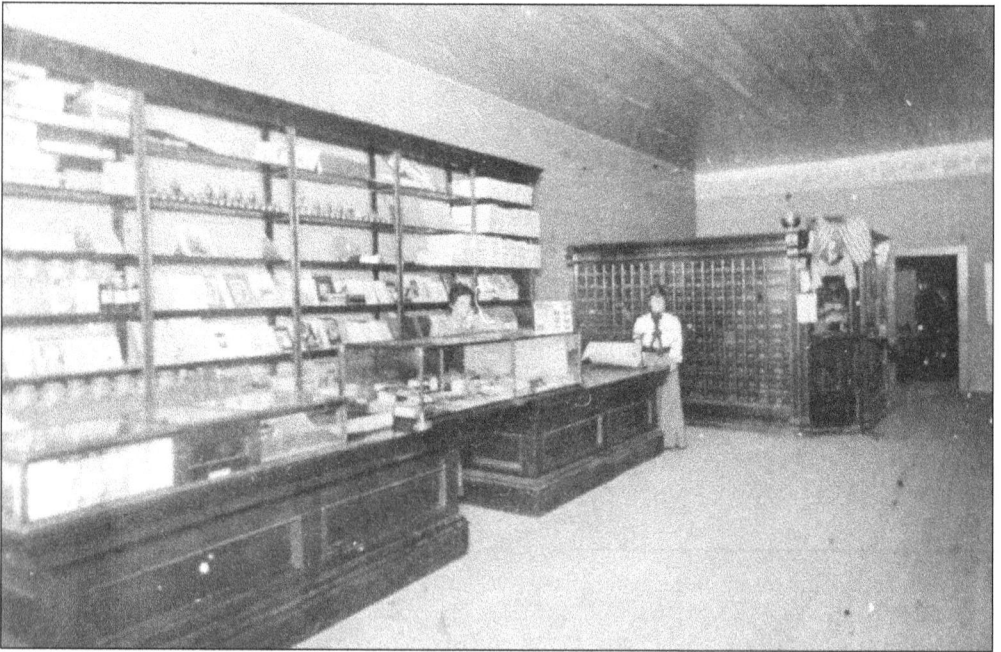

KENNEWICK POST OFFICE IN 1904. Mrs. William Morsin is in the rear of the photo. The post office was in the back of the Morain Store. The city was growing, as was evidenced by the expanded school enrollment. The post office was enlarged this year and Miss Jarnagan, Miss Florence Oliver, and Miss Peckinpaugh were appointed deputies. (Courtesy of EBCHS.)

SADIE CONWAY IN FRONT OF CONWAY'S POST OFFICE AND STORE. An 1892 issue of the *Gazette* listed Kennewick, the former post office of Tehe, a population of 25. It listed Sadie and her husband Charles Conway, who was postmaster, express, telegraph, and railway agent, as business people. The Conways came to Kennewick in 1888. Joseph Dimond was postmaster in 1885. In 1884 he built the first business structure in Kennewick—a general merchandising store from which he catered to the railroad employees. On November 11, 1885, Nora Knowlton became postmistress. The position went to A.R. Leeper next. From November of 1888 to May of 1889 the postmaster was V.G. Savage. Conway stated that a young woman was postmistress when he and his wife came to Kennewick; possibly this was Nora Knowlton. She gave the position to the storekeeper, probably A.R. Leeper. This person passed the job on to Conway in about 1892. (Courtesy of EBCHS.)

MAIL DELIVERY IN 1907. The R.A. Oliver family is shown here in the first auto to deliver Kennewick's mail. R.A. was the first carrier on rural Route #1, which started in February of 1907 when the post office was moved to new quarters in the Williams building just north of the Hampshire House. In 1905, R.A. Oliver was one of Kennewick's top strawberry growers. (Courtesy of EBCHS.)

THE OLD KENNEWICK CITY HALL, BUILT IN 1906. It is shown here in 1966, shortly before it was destroyed by fire. Along with getting a new city hall in 1906, Kennewick's post office was upgraded to third class in January. The postmaster also took on the responsibility of the official weather station. It was the first and only one in Benton County. (Courtesy of EBCHS.)

Seven

GETTING HERE
AND THERE

LONE RIDER THROUGH KENNEWICK. The near empty street seen here with a lone horseback rider ambling along gives a small hint of wild western days not long gone by, nor quite forgotten. Attesting to the fact that Kennewick is ready to launch into the future are the power poles along the street, their wires lining the skyline high above board walkway. (Courtesy of EBCHS.)

R.H. RIBLET AND DAUGHTER VIRGINIA IN 1897 WITH THEIR BICYCLES. By 1900 bicycle riding was popular. You could order a bicycle from Sears, Roebuck, and Company. Their fall catalogue for 1900 offered several models. For the sum of $13.75 you could purchase their New Model Acme Jewel. This was a man's bike and offered a choice of three frame sizes. Or for the grand total of $15.75 you could choose from either the Celebrated Gents' Acme King or the New Model Ladies Acme Queen bicycle. The catalogue stated that at the above "special" price Sears would furnish these two bicycles complete with handle bars, saddle, dress guard in the case of a ladies' bike, combination pedals, tool bag, and all necessary tools for repairs. That bicycling was becoming popular was evident, one year after the above photo was taken, by a 6-day "Go as You Please" race in Madison Square Garden where Charlie Miller pedaled 2,093 miles. It was reported that so many of his rivals were hospitalized for exhaustion that a public outcry nearly ended the race. (Courtesy of EBCHS.)

AND YOU THOUGHT TRAFFIC WAS BUSY TODAY! This is a street in Kennewick in the early 1900s. If it was getting too dusty in town from the traffic, in 1911, you could join the 400 boosters who went on the river excursion backed by the Commercial Club. They chartered two steamers and visited all the towns between Kennewick and White Bluffs to secure cooperation in promoting local products. (Courtesy of EBCHS.)

GETTING HERE AND THERE IN 1906? Maybe you could with snowshoes. This is the way Kennewick looked during the winter of 1906, looking towards the Methodist Church, visible on the left. Even without the snow the rural mail delivery was having a difficult time getting through in 1906 due to the lack of roads and the poor condition of those that did exist. (Courtesy of EBCHS.)

FRANK EMIGH WITH A WAGON LOADED WITH BERRY CRATES. Frank is pictured here in 1906 in front of the H.M. Ashbaugm and Company Dry Goods. The unusually high temperatures in July of this year helped not only the berry crops to grow, but also all produce. In August there was a second crop of strawberries nearly as heavy as the first. Watermelons did exceptionally well, too. (Courtesy of EBCHS.)

MERRY CHRISTMAS 1908. The flag-waving occasion for this gathering of unidentified Kennewick folks on the banks of the Columbia River was to produce a photograph for a Christmas card entitled "Greetings to the Inland Empire." Going to church was always a fine place to drive to. In this year a new Congregational Church was added to all the other religious establishments in Kennewick. (Courtesy of EBCHS.)

WAITING FOR THE TRAIN, c. 1905. This was a great way to travel but it could have its drawbacks. On September 14, 1905 a passenger train and a freight train smashed head-on in the early morning hours. Fortunately, no one was injured and no damage was done to the coaches. The headlight and pilot were knocked off of the passenger engine, however. (Courtesy of EBCHS.)

THE HARRY BEACH FAMILY, OUT FOR A BUGGY RIDE IN 1910. By this year there were several new places you could take a ride to. On July 6th work began on the Celilo Canal. It was a project sure to draw considerable interest. The first movie house in Kennewick also opened this year, offering shows twice a week. (Courtesy of EBCHS.)

KING'S DELIVERY TRUCK IN 1910. This was King's first auto used for delivery service. In front of the store to the far left is W.G. King. His son Clarence E. King is in the auto. By 1907, King and Son had moved into its new department store building. It was finished in mission style, and had prism-lighted show windows on both Pacific and Second Streets. (Courtesy of EBCHS.)

MIXING CONCRETE. Pictured here is C.H. Boyles posing with his four horse-drawn, Koehring Concrete mixers, and 18 unidentified men. The men and their equipment are on their way to cement six-and-a-half miles of canal for the lower Yakima Irrigation Company in 1910. In this year, Jessie Sonderman got to take an automobile ride in one of the first autos in Kennewick. (Courtesy of EBCHS)

A TWO-SEATER BUGGY IN 1911. Mrs. Pratt, Mabel Barimone, Myra, and Carol are pictured here. In this year, officials of the Oregon, Washington Railroad and Navigation Company came on a "seeing Kennewick" auto tour. In March it was determined that state highways were to converge in Kennewick. It was hoped that the state would build a bridge over the Columbia. (Courtesy of EBCHS.)

ELMER FERGUSON AND HIS SPORTS CAR IN 1915. By 1896 there were 16 cars in use in the U.S. By 1906 over a hundred thousand autos were cruising around the country. When Elmer bought his sports car he might have been dreaming of the famous race that had taken place for the first time in 1911, the Memorial Day race at Indianapolis Speedway. (Courtesy of EBCHS.)

NO AUTO OR BUGGY NEEDED HERE. Charles and Bell Robertson, brother and sister, are out for a horseback ride in 1915. Note that Bell is riding sidesaddle. River traffic had a big boost this year with the opening of the Celilo Canal after ten years of work and a cost of $4.85 million in government money. During its construction, 1,500 men were employed. (Courtesy of EBCHS.)

CLARENCE KING ON THE JOB. King is shown here working for the Pacific Power and Light Company. He was with them from 1918 to 1919. Clarence is believed to be the gentleman on the left seated on the wagon. There wasn't much travel for pleasure in 1918 as there was a severe flu epidemic on. Churches, schools, and theaters were closed on October 10th. (Courtesy of EBCHS.)

THIS COULD HAVE BEEN A PARADE OF AUTOMOBILES, BUT IT WASN'T. These well-wheeled folks are taking a tour of R.E. Pratt's hog farm. By 1921 Kennewick folks were seeing many more cars on their streets. It was about this time that the state began requiring all drivers to have licenses. A favorite place to drive to was the Highlands Club House where dances were held. (Courtesy of EBCHS.)

GOING FOR A SUNDAY DRIVE IN 1922. Charles Hall and family pose here with their Dodge Touring car. From left to right are Fred Hall, Bud, Bill, Mrs. Charles Hall, Kitty, her daughter Leona, and Charles Hall's mother. They may have used the new bridge between Kennewick and Pasco. Some folks didn't, due to the 75¢-a-car toll that was charged to cross it. (Courtesy of EBCHS.)

KENNEWICK-PASCO AUTO BRIDGE NEARS COMPLETION. The last piece of the bridge was put into place in September of 1922. The bridge completion meant that both Kennewick and Pasco could now more swiftly roll into the future. Sadly for many, it also meant the passing of an era and the demise of the ferry service that had served so well for many years. (Courtesy of EBCHS.)

FIRST OVER THE NEW AUTO BRIDGE. This photo was taken on October 5, 1922, shortly after the Auto Bridge linking Kennewick and Pasco across the Columbia was finished. Shown from left to right is T.O. Webster; Charles J. Huber, construction manager; Capt. W.P. Gray, a former riverboat pilot; and P.J. O'Brien, construction superintendent. Later, many just drove over and then turned around and came back. (Courtesy of EBCHS.)

GET A HORSE, MISTER! This was the usual taunt from those that were certain that motorcars were only a passing fad. The "fad" stuck just as these unidentified motorists are certainly stuck until the man at the top of the picture, headed down the muddy hill with his horses, can pry their auto out of the muck and send them on their way. (Courtesy of EBCHS.)

JOHN NEUMAN DELIVERING GROCERIES IN A MODEL A FORD IN 1923. Driving autos in and around Kennewick this year may have been a pleasure until winter hit. In January, Kennewick experienced one of the worst windstorms ever. Trees were uprooted, windows were broken, and 25 poles went down. In February, roads to the west were blocked by snow, and even the trains were stalled. (Courtesy of EBCHS.)

Gas at 30¢ a Gallon in 1924! That was the price advertised that year at Beste's Tire Shop. Beste's offered U.S. Tires and Royal and Nobby Cords with water and air at the curb while you filled up your tank at the pump. As a side attraction they also offered shoe repairing. Butt's jewelry store is next door. Beyond it was the theater. (Courtesy of EBCHS.)

The Last Ride, But in Grand Style. Pictured here is I.N. Muller's new hearse he purchased in 1907. Mueller came to Kennewick in the early 1900s from Iowa. He was first employed here by Ed Howe as a mortician and plumber. In 1909 he married Annie Caroline Amon. In 1910 they established the first Mueller Funeral Home, located in the King Block at Kennewick Avenue and Cascade. (Courtesy of EBCHS.)

Eight

GROWING UP
WITH KENNEWICK

LOCUST STREET SCHOOL IN 1910. It was also know as the Amon School House, located on the southeast corner of Locust and Nicosin Roads. The Locust Grove Grange met in the school building from 1917 through 1930. In 1936 the school district was disorganized. In 1996 the building, with the bell tower, could still be seen from Locust Grove Road. (Courtesy of EBCHS.)

THE AMON CHILDREN IN 1889. Seen here are Will, Ruth (Williams), Alfred, and Annie (Mueller). Their father was W.R. Amon who was born in Missouri on February 26, 1846 and came to Washington in 1890. Their mother was Sarah Melvina (Downing). Alfred and Will farmed in the Horse Haven Hills. Alfred ran the Farmer's Exchange from 1923 to 1952 and was mayor of Kennewick in his later years. (Courtesy of EBCHS.)

NORTH SCHOOL IN 1894. It was located at the corner of Entiat and Fruitland Streets, the present-day location of Fruitland Park. In 1896, a break in the irrigation ditch caused a water shut-down with no money for repairs. Though many settlers moved on, some stuck it out. Gus Pearson was one of those who stayed. His sons Bill and Henry attended school in Kennewick during the slow times. (Courtesy of EBCHS.)

VAN MARTIN AND FRANK RICHARDS AS YOUNG BOYS IN 1896. They are seated on the woodpile in a back yard. These two young fellows appear to be enjoying life in Kennewick. It can only be wondered if they participated in the measles epidemic that hit Kennewick in February of 1899. The Richards family was some of the earliest pioneers to settle in Kennewick. (Courtesy of EBCHS.)

KENNEWICK SCHOOL DAYS IN 1896. Sitting on the fence at the old North School, from left to right, are John Richards, Ella Martin, Bill Martin, Van Martin, Bertha Richards, and Frank Richards. Though many settlers were leaving Kennewick about this time because of lack of water for crops, Bill and Van Martin were two that stuck it out to grow up with Kennewick. (Courtesy of EBCHS.)

PRETTY ENOUGH TO BE THE PIN-UP GIRL FOR 1897. Virginia Riblet is pictured here with her bicycle. A few years after this photo was taken irrigation water arrived in Kennewick. The population began to grow, so it is expected that Virginia had lots of new playmates to grow up with. There were also two doctors in town, by 1902, to keep little girls healthy. (Courtesy of EBCHS.)

TEACHER MOLLY MORGAN AND HER 1899 CLASS. These unidentified children probably attended the North School that was built in 1894. Just how many children were attending school at this time is undetermined but the 1892 issue of the *Gazeteer* gave Kennewick a population of 25. However, four years later when the irrigation project shut down, many settlers left for wetter pastures. (Courtesy of EBCHS.)

TOM SAWYER IN KENNEWICK? No, it's
Odin Staley as a boy, in 1904, during
strawberry season. Staley's talents went
from strawberry packing to making
repairs on the burned roof of Mrs. Lucy
Willsey's boarding house in 1923. In
1932, during the Depression, Odin
teamed up with C.C. Williams and
C.A. Carpenter during Kennewick's
chest drive to solicit cash donations for
local relief work. (Courtesy of EBCHS.)

KENNEWICK SCHOOL IN 1905. Included here are all four grades. Pictured here, left to right, are:
(front row) Fracy Howe, Clint Oliver, Everett Howe, Roy Larkin, Earl Barham, Henry Tweedt,
Guy Story, Roger Woods, unidentified, ? Barham, and unidentified; (back row) Ethel Tompkin,
Alfred Moor, Molly Godfrey, Ceney Sercombe, Mabel Howe, Floyd Haxton, Mattie Waterman,
Nima Hoodley, Audrey Fullerton, Bernice Griffith, Mae Sercombe, Effie Howe, Erma Caka,
and Ellen Richardson. (Courtesy of EBCHS.)

WASHINGTON STREET SCHOOL, BUILT IN 1907. Unlike Kennewick's first school, this one did not burn down. Other school buildings were not so fortunate. In 1903, Mrs. Caroline Klitten bought the Columbia Hotel from the Northern Pacific Railroad and established the Emanuel Academy there. It was open only a few months when Mrs. Klitten's $30,000 investment went up in smoke. (Courtesy of EBCHS.)

KENNEWICK SCHOOL BUS IN 1909. This was one of Kennewick's first school buses, shown here on River Road. By 1904 many children lived out in Horse Heaven and in the Highlands, and C.H. Putnam obtained the contract to bus the children to school. G.W. Barnes bused the children living on the west route. Marshall Glover was the truant officer. C. Vertrees was the principal. (Courtesy of EBCHS.)

KENNEWICK'S FIRST GRADUATING CLASS, 1908. Seated in the front row, left to right, are Jay Perry, Audrey Fullerton, Lloyd Haxton, and Guy Story, not pictured. In the back row are Fannie Smith, Nima Hoadly, Mae Sercombe, and Ethel Thompkins. At the commencement, Fullerton read her paper on Kennewick's school history, beginning in 1884. Perry, having come to Kennewick in 1904, later recalled jackrabbits running through the sagebrush. Haxton's family farm was included with those producing large crops of strawberries in 1905. Sports were of interest to Story, who was on the 1909 football team. Smith was one of those listed, in 1907, as best all-around students. In 1911 Hoadley was crowned Queen of that year's First Annual Grape Festival. In 1938 the Sercombe's family was honored as one of Kennewick's first families. The Sercombes came to Kennewick in 1902. As these graduates grew up, not all events were joyous. In 1928 Ethel Tomkins' invalid mother drowned herself in the irrigation canal. At that time, Ethel was Mrs. Dusair. (Courtesy of EBCHS.)

KENNEWICK IN 1909. In this year a public library became more than just a dream. Edna Dimmick was the first librarian and many books were donated. In May, the local wine was declared outstanding and someone predicted that it was equal to Europe's best. But not all was wine and books. In August typhoid struck and temporary hospitals had to be quickly arranged. (Courtesy of EBCHS.)

HOWARD AND ELNA BESTE IN 1909. They are pictured here in the harness shop of Frank Beste of Kennewick. In 1924, Howard graduated from high school with honors. He went on to be one of 49 students from Benton County to attend Washington State College. Local fame came to Elna, in 1933, when she was voted the best local redhead in the "Coppercapped Queen Contest." (Courtesy of EBCHS.)

THREE OF THE SONDERMAN CHILDREN, ABOUT 1911. Pictured here are Josie, Julie, and Bud. They are the children of Willis Sonderman and Effie Aune Sonderman, and grandchildren of Kennewick pioneer Charles Aune. One of Effie's best friends in Kennewick was the daughter of an Indian family that lived in a wigwam near the Aune's home. Effie Aune married Willis Sonderman when she was 15. (Courtesy of EBCHS.)

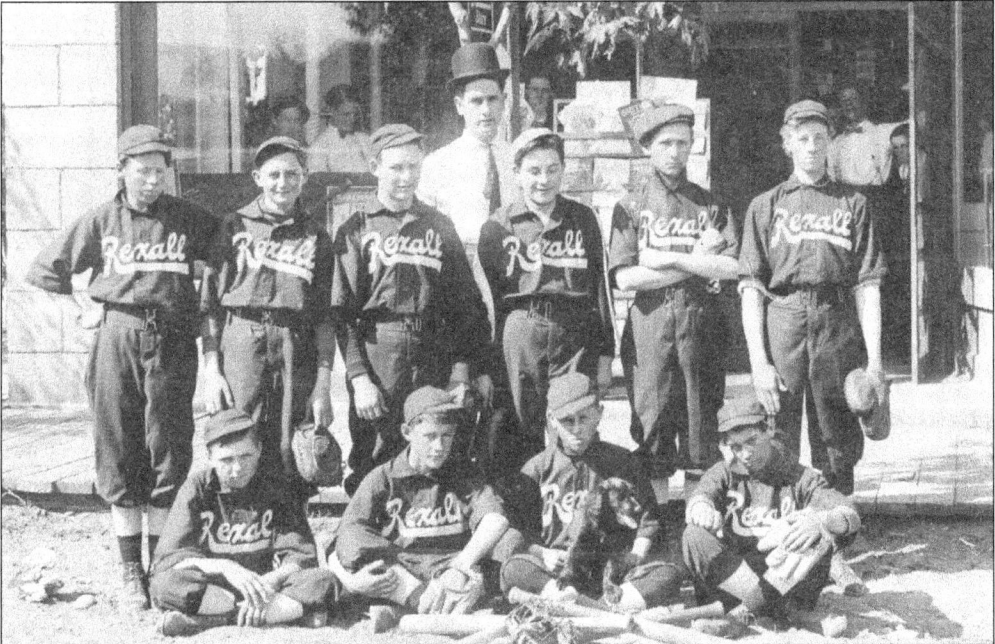

BATTER UP! In 1910 Rexall Drugs sponsored this boys baseball team. The unidentified team members and their equipment are posing in front of Tulles Drug Company. The first Tulles Drug Store was in the Eakin Building at the northeastern corner of present-day Kennewick Avenue and Cascade. As early as 1906 the Horse Heaven Hustler baseball team was taking on the Kennewick Sand Snufflers. (Courtesy of EBCHS.)

THE MOULTON SISTERS. All dressed up are Ester Moulton (Mrs. Knowles), Helen Moulton (Mrs. Connell), and Margaret Moulton (Mrs. Galligan). Their parents were Mark and Ester Moulton. In 1915 Ester was a flower girl during a mock wedding celebrating the opening of Celilo Canal. In 1926, Helen graduated from Kennewick High School, and Margaret graduated in 1930. (Courtesy of EBCHS.)

KENNEWICK HIGH SCHOOL'S GRADUATING CLASS OF 1915. Pictured, left to right, are: (front row) Orlin Fisher, Hinnie Witt, Bill Roseway, Beulah Puhler, Dorothy Wright, Bernard (?), unidentified, and Margaret (?); (back row) Buck Art Simsiu, unidentified, John Hamilton, Ralph Dague, Alice Baxter, Glads Dague, and Bill Schuster. Orlin Fisher married Lylan Norene Halliday, who graduated in 1919. (Courtesy of EBCHS.)

THE GRAVENSLUNDS, A FAMILY WHO GREW UP WITH KENNEWICK. And they continue to grow with Kennewick. Pictured above are Wilma, Richard, and John Gravenslund, the children of Zella and Wilmont Gravenslund. Wilmont was the son of John Hans Gravenslund. John, above, bought Washington Hardware. The business is still owned by the Gravenslund family. Today, it is run by John Gravenslund Jr., John's son. (Courtesy of EBCHS.)

THE GILES CHILDREN. From left to right are Howard, Merlin, Warren, Bergman, and Lorraine. Their parents, Fred and Emma, arrived in 1911 with baby Lorraine. They homesteaded 10 acres that is now the section on 4th Avenue between Union and Edison Streets. Lorraine graduated from Kennewick High School in 1936, followed by Bergman in 1938. Warren graduated in 1941 and Merlin in 1942. (Courtesy of EBCHS.)

First Grade at Washington School in 1920. Miss Anderson was the teacher. The school was located at what is now Keewaydin Plaza on 6th Avenue in Kennewick. Posing for a class picture are, left to right: (first row) Margaret Frinboth, Evelyn Larkin, Eunice Foraker, Jane ?, and the others are unidentified; (second row) Elsie Gleason, Dorothy Burkman, John Whitney, Pauline Shriver, Lester Foraker, two unidentified, Bertha Higgenbuttom, and two unidentified; (third row) unidentified, Sammy Schuster, unidentified, and Ed Faulds; (fourth row) three unidentified, Arthur Glassow, four unidentified, and Audrey Sweeney. Those who graduated from Kennewick High School in 1932 were Lester Foraker, Elsie Gleason, and Eunice Foraker, who was valedictorian. Eunice held leading roles in two school plays: the 1931 junior class play "The Gypsy Trail" and the 1932 senior class play "Hobson's Choice." Art Glasow graduated in 1933 and Ed Faulds in 1934. The year, 1920, that these children started their education was the birth-year of Kennewick High School's annual "The Keewaydin." Jessie Sonderman, who graduated that year, was instrumental in its naming. (Courtesy of EBCHS.)

116

Nine

WAR AND MORE

ARMY MEN FROM KENNEWICK. Pictured from left to right, first names unknown, are Gill, Lawrence, Shauman, Kisichi, Knight, and Huff. When President Wilson declared war against Germany, the U.S. only had a small army, but by August of 1918, the American First Army of over half a million men had gone into operation as a unit under the command of General John J. Pershing. (Courtesy of EBCHS.)

PHIL SCHIREMAN IN UNIFORM. Before Schireman entered the military, several things had occurred. In 1914 Austria-Hungary declared war on Serbia, and then Germany declared war on Russia. Less than a year later, a German submarine torpedoed an American vessel, the *SS Gulflight*, killing two Americans. Six days later, at about 2 p.m. and without warning, the German U-boat Number 20 loosed a torpedo from a range of 700 meters. The shot was a score, hitting the starboard side of its target just abaft of the bridge. Within 22 minutes, located at the southern-most point of Ireland, the *Lusitania* slipped, bow first, beneath the waves, taking 1,198 passengers and crew to their deaths. Among the dead were 124 Americans. When, on March 22, 1917, the newspapers declared that "a state of war now exists between the U.S. and Germany," citizens in the Kennewick Valley began entertaining trainloads of boys going off to Camp Green, Nebraska. Battery B was the unit that contained the early volunteers from Kennewick and Richland. World War I had begun. (Courtesy of EBCHS.)

ODIN STALEY IN 1917. Throughout the war, Staley's humor never failed, to the delight of the folks who read his letters to his friend "Bat," that were published in the *Courier-Reporter*. In one letter, Staley, who was known as Dutch, requested a corncob pipe if he was expected to lick the Kaiser. Home folks were responsive and Dutch received 16 Missouri Meerschaums in one week. (Courtesy of EBCHS.)

WORN WITH PRIDE. This U.S. Army uniform jacket is displayed with the ever-needed water canteen slung over one shoulder. In Northern France, a French officer observed the unique Army and Marine forces being led by Pershing and commented: "The good God, Himself, could not stop those men." His words were proven true on November 11, 1918, when Germany agreed to lay down its arms. (Courtesy of EBCHS.)

119

CARL AUNE. This younger brother of Effie Sonderman was born sometime after 1887, prior to the Aunes moving onto their homestead east of Kennewick. When Carl enlisted perhaps he recalled his father, Charles Aune, helping Captain Lum erect a flagpole for the new flag that was raised at Kennewick's first July 4th celebration in 1890, commemorating Washington State's admission to the Union in 1889. (Courtesy of EBCHS.)

HARRY AUNE. It is believed that Harry was a brother of Carl Aune and Effie Aune Sonderman. If so, he may have remembered the Aune's home that stood near the Old Military Road that followed the bank of the Columbia River. He also may have watched the cavalry travel through the area on their way from Walla Walla to camp at American Lake. (Courtesy of EBCHS.)

LARRY OLIVER IN HIS MARINE UNIFORM DURING WWI. Five others joined the Marines. They were William Sly, Elwin Brace, Howard Paul, Perry Soth, and Howard O'Dell. Larry evidently returned from the war unharmed because it is recorded that in 1935 he managed to break both arms. He fell from the roof of his barbershop while attempting to install a sprinkler on the roof. (Courtesy of EBCHS.)

THE PURPLE HEART PRESENTED TO PAUL O. STONE. It was awarded to him for military merit in the Army during World War I. Stone graduated from the University of Oregon Dentist School, receiving his D.D.S., in 1928. In 1929, he married Ida Womack of Farmville, Virginia and practiced dentistry in Lind, Washington from 1928–1930. At that time he came to Kennewick, where he retired in 1945. (Courtesy of EBCHS.)

CHARLES SONDERMAN IN HIS WORLD WAR I UNIFORM. Another war was raging around the world at the same time—the war against influenza. In October 1918, throughout the U.S, the death rate from the epidemic reached 202 deaths daily. The French said it had started in Spain and the Spanish blamed it on France. The Americans were certain it came from Eastern Europe. In spite of its origin, in the 46 states, almost 500,000 died before it ran its course in 1919. It was a total that nearly tripled the amount of deaths of those that were killed by influenza during World War I. Approximately 130,000 cases alone raged through 20 Army camps, killing about half as many as died in combat in France. In Kennewick, schools, theaters, and churches were closed on October 10, 1918. On December 12, 95 new cases were reported. Many Kennewick citizens died. Among them were Fred Kadow Jr. and T.E. Golden. Charles Sonderman, born February 17, 1896, was the son of Effie Aune Sonderman and Willis Sonderman. (Courtesy of EBCHS.)

ZELA GRAVENSLUND, WWI RED CROSS
VOLUNTEER. In 1881 Clara Barton
organized the American Association of
the Red Cross and by 1900, there were
national Red Cross societies in nearly 30
countries. When the U.S. entered World
War I, the Red Cross quickly expanded
to 3,700 chapters with 20 million members, two of which were Kennewick's Zela
Gravenslund and Amy Bartlett, who went
to France. (Courtesy of EBCHS.)

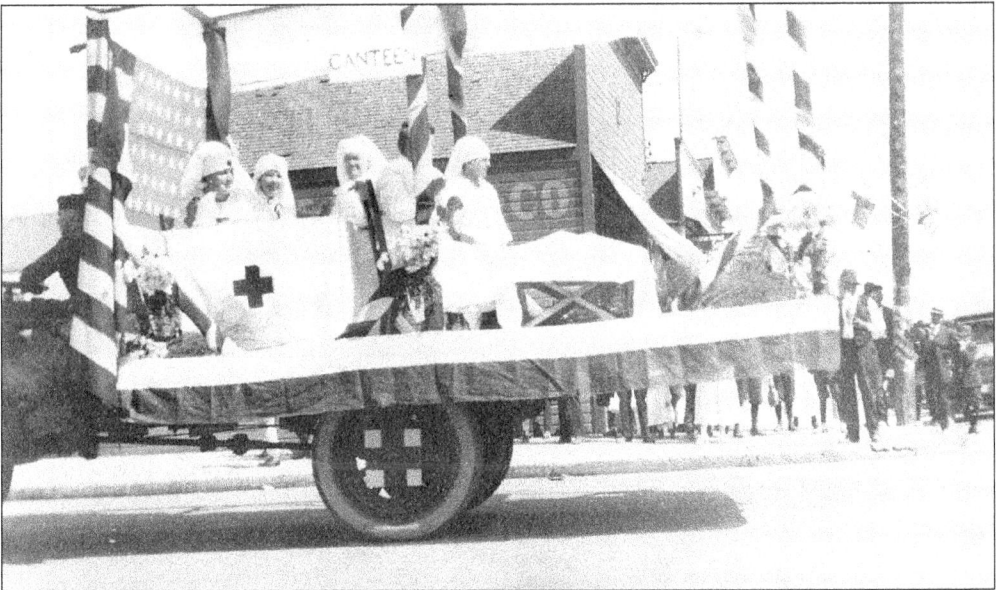

RED CROSS WOMEN IN THE ARMISTICE DAY PARADE, 1922. They had much to celebrate. Back
in January of 1918 Kennewick learned that the 146th Field Artillery was safe in France. Then
on February 7 the news came that Battery B boys were in England with F.R. Jeffreys and Sgt.
Fred Berg. The end of the war came on November 11, 1918. (Courtesy of EBCHS.)

YOU'RE IN THE NAVY NOW, NOT BEHIND THE PLOW. For Frank Shaughnessy, who played the drums for the Kennewick band in 1907, that musical line came true during the war. The inscription on his hatband, an item that came to be termed a "Donald Duck hat" and is no longer issued, indicates Frank served aboard the USS *Illinois*. On March 17, 1916, German submarines sank five American merchantmen. The following month Shaugnessy's ship may have been among those that received the message the Navy radio station at Arlington clicked out to all ships and stations: "The President has signed an act of Congress which declares that a state of war exists between the United States and Germany." In August Congress passed the Naval Act, a five-year building program authorizing the construction of 205 naval vessels and enough personnel to man existing ships. This number included 100 submarines. President Wilson, who had at first declared the U.S. a neutral country, now wanted the best naval fleet in the world. (Courtesy of EBCHS.)

ORLIN FISHER SERVED HIS COUNTRY IN THE U.S. NAVY. He is pictured here on the left in what appears to be his dress blue uniform. With him are his parents, Mr. and Mrs. Fisher. Orlin returned to Kennewick after the war and in 1922 married Lylyan Halliday, who had moved to Kennewick in 1914. The Fishers came to Kennewick in 1904. (Courtesy of EBCHS.)

SHE'S A GRAND OLD FLAG. This is the Armistice Day Parade that took place on November 11, 1918. The view is looking east from the corner of Kennewick Avenue and Washington Street. In February, reports of troop ships being torpedoed by German subs was frightening to the folks back home in Kennewick. A troop transport was sunk, but the news came that our local boys were safe. (Courtesy of EBCHS.)

"FLY WITH FLOYD." This was the slogan that advertised Kennewick's first airplane, owned by Floyd Kelso. Of all those returning from the war, Kelso's was the most colorful when he landed his plane right in Kennewick. Later, on July 31, 1919, Floyd and his bride, the former Miss Gladys Hundall, were married in the "flying field" hangar. They then flew off on their honeymoon. (Courtesy of EBCHS.)

ODIN STALEY AND HIS BRIDE GEORGIA IN 1919. Odin and Georgia had one son, Kenneth, born in June of 1920. When war was declared between the U.S. and Germany, Staley may have been one of the first to volunteer or he may have been one of the draftees selected on Lottery Day on July 20, 1917 when 2,702,687 men were finally sworn into the Army. (Courtesy of EBCHS.)

CAPT. JOHN W. VICKERS AND HIS FAMILY. Pictured in front, from left to right, are Mrs. Vickers and six-year-old Gladys. Standing is John Vickers, owner of the Highland Fruit Company Ranch Number 1. When World War I started Captain Vickers helped organized a branch of the Spokane Fruit Growers and after hours was out with eight squadrons, drilling them as soldiers. When the war was over Vickers continued to be a significant part of Kennewick. In 1922 he was instrumental in helping raise the additional money needed to complete the new Methodist church and assisted in reviving the Lyceum Circuit's return to Kennewick. By 1925, with World War I in the past, Vickers and other local persons farmed "Vista Orchards," with the purchase of 40 acres to plant in the Highlands. Vickers' daughter Gladys became a famous woman pilot and in 1935 was regaled as Kennewick's Hometown Aviatrix when she performed stunt flying as part of the July 4th celebration. By 1937 Gladys and her husband Ed Cooks had established a school of aviation in Kennewick. (Courtesy of EBCHS.)

KENNEWICK, ALL GROWN UP IN 1925. The new mayor, J.C. Liebee, appointed Wilmont Gravenslund fire chief with Albert Haas as his assistant. The Community Club requested more lights on Main Street. City streets were renamed for better service with mail delivery and every business and every house had a number. Main Street was renamed Kennewick Avenue. North-south streets were named for trees east of Washington Street. Those streets to the west were named for pioneers, and all in alphabetical order. By August the town park was ready for the 614 students growing up in this bountiful desert. Someday these children would start businesses and farms and raise families of their own. They would make the land flourish with orchards and vineyards. There would be fun times on the rivers and more wars. Many of them would leave descendants who would hear that lonesome whistle in the deep hours of the night as the train passed through town. But most of all they would make a place to call home in Kennewick, Washington. (Courtesy of EBCHS.)

www.ingramcontent.com/pod-product-compliance
Lightning Source LLC
Chambersburg PA
CBHW050642110426
42813CB00007B/1888